The Midlife Crisis
of a Nineteen-Year-Old

The Midlife Crisis
OF A Nineteen-Year-Old

HUNTER CARTER

LUMINARE PRESS
WWW.LUMINAREPRESS.COM

The Midlife Crisis of a Nineteen-Year-Old
Copyright © 2024 by Hunter Carter

All rights reserved. This book or any portion thereof may not be reproduced or used in any manner whatsoever without the express written permission of the publisher, except for the use of brief quotations in a book review.

Printed in the United States of America

Luminare Press
442 Charnelton St.
Eugene, OR 97401
www.luminarepress.com

LCCN: 2023918217
ISBN: 979-8-88679-392-5

To Poppies

PROLOGUE

My name is Hunter. This story is about me and the friends I grew up with and how we are now twenty years old and think we rule the world. Little did we know the world rules us, and sometimes it really fuckin' sucks.

CHAPTER 1

Where It All Started

There was a kid, and just for the sake of not getting in trouble for using his name, we'll call him Jukes. Jukes would set up these football games at 32nd, which is a football field, every once in a blue moon. I didn't go to a lot of them, but when I did go, I would invite my friends—we'll get to them later. Once we got to the football field there were a lot of people we knew. The two who stood out the most were the two kids we used to go to school with. They transferred to another school a couple years ago called Mohawk High School. This school is in a small town called Marcola. I used to go to Marcola all the time when I was a kid so I was pretty familiar with it. So, I forgot to tell you a big part of the story—these kids that we knew I used to play football with freshman year of high school, and after that I never played again. OK, so now that you're all caught up, let's get back to the story. As we're playing this football game, they looked at me and my friends, and finally they asked the question that would change our lives forever: "Why don't you guys transfer out to Mohawk? It would be fuckin' awesome!" I know for a fact we all went home that day thinking about all of the possibilities that would happen if we transferred and how it would change our lives.

The next day at school, we all sat at one of the little round tables in the middle of Thurston High School's cafeteria, except it wasn't like usual. It was more like a business meeting we were having. One of my friends finally said, "So, guys what do you think about what they said?" I don't think any of us said it but deep inside all of us were saying: "Yeah that's fuckin' nuts. That shit is not happening." A little "Yeah, I think that'd be pretty cool" came out of me and Kade; well, Kade didn't really have an opinion. Ohhh, fuck me, I completely forgot to tell you my buddies' names. Well, just hold out and I'll explain all of them. As we were still sitting at the table, I think Dalton said: "It's crazy, but why not do it? I mean none of us like Thurston. It's just we've been going here our whole lives so why stop right before senior year." I've never agreed to anything more in my entire life.

Now, all of us knew what we wanted to do, but we still needed a plan, and we still needed to go over it with our other friend who wasn't even at school that day. As we were coming up with a plan, the bell rang to go to class. We all rushed to class, and for the rest of the day, none of us could focus on school. All we were focused on was how in the hell are we gonna get into that school.

A day goes by, and weeks go by, and it's almost like all of us forgot about the plan and the whole idea in the first place. Finally, one day we were all hanging out, and that's when someone asked Brody—the kid who wasn't at school the day we were talking about it—what he thought about transferring out to Mohawk. He thought the whole idea was good, but he said it would never work because of our parents. We were all so excited about the plan and everything that we forgot about the most important part—talking to the parents. What kind of fucking idiots forget about something that huge? Oh, that's right, us. Anyway, when we finally finished the plan, that night all of us would sit down and talk with our parents all at the same time. All of our parents were close. So if one of us said something that crazy, then they would most likely contact the other parent to see what was going on. The talk I had with my parents was pretty quick. I told them that for my senior year I wanted to transfer out to Mohawk High School, and just when they were about to say no, I said, "Oh yeah, also Brody, Dalton, and Kade want to go there too." Those were the magic words. My mom called Dalton's mom, and they both thought the idea was batshit crazy. But they said that if that's what we wanted to do, then we could do it.

We still had a pretty good amount of time until senior year started, but I started to tell the kids we used to go to school with that we were coming out there. As I was texting with one of the kids, he brought up a training camp for football that they had this upcoming week. The camp lasts for about a month or something like that, until actual practice for football starts. As soon as he said football, I was hooked. I talked to the guys and we went, but Kade couldn't go because, well, Kade is pretty much a complete idiot. Dalton's words, not mine.

Once we got there it was pretty weird. When you go somewhere not knowing a single soul out there except for the two people you talked to and the people you show up with, it's pretty damn weird. As we got there, people looked us up and down, left to right. Shit, if you can think of it, they probably did it. We had to fill out some paperwork before we could do the camp. As we're filling out the paperwork, we notice a kid who looks familiar. Turns out, he also goes to Thurston. The only thing is this kid is a complete douche. I want you to do me a favor, think of the douche at your school. OK, now double that and you have this kid. I remember the kid looked at me and said, "Oh, hey second string." As soon as he said those words, I was more determined than ever to play well. It almost felt like the draft combine, these coaches have never seen us or heard of us, so we want to make sure we do really well. I won't get into too much detail of how the camp went, but let's just say we were drafted in the first round. Oh, also, that douche, he was a complete trash can, probably the worst QB I've ever seen. Let me tell ya, that was pretty damn funny to see!

Anyway, I got off track there a little bit. Let's get back to it. So, after that day of the training camp, the coach talked to all of us and asked if we were transferring out to Mohawk, and all of us were pretty certain about it, so we said yes! Later that night, my parents were taking everyone back to their homes. First was Brody's house. Brody said his dad still needed some convincing if he was going to go to the school, so my mom walked up with Brody to the door. As the rest of us were in the truck, we just saw hands flying every which way, and then my mom and Brody's dad just staring at Brody, and then my mom came back to the truck. When she got to the truck, we asked her what that was all about, and, well, this is by far one of the dumbest things Brody has ever done. *He never told his dad about Mohawk!* We all thought we had a plan and everyone knew what was going on, but little did we know diptard Brody didn't even tell his parents!

The next day we went back to the camp but this time without Brody. The coach asked us what happened. We told him and he basically had the same response as us. What an idiot! At this point, Dalton and I are thinking there's no point in even going with the plan anymore because everything was falling apart. All of a sudden, the miracle that we needed finally happened. One of the coaches went to Brody's work and talked to him. This interested Brody's dad so they took a tour of the school, which was about a few steps of walking, and his dad enjoyed it, so he said Brody was able to come out. Now we're back in business, baby!

Dalton and I were going on a hunting trip so we were going to miss the rest of the camp and a few of the first practices. So when we got back, we had to do little workouts with some of the other people who missed the practices too. When we got back, we started going to the practices, and that's when we met Zeke. This kid played lacrosse and was crazy fast! There was also another kid coming, and we met him at the camp, and his name was Kay. This is a day I'll remember for the rest of my life. When a truck pulled up to drop off Kay, I looked at who was driving, and I turned to Zeke and said, "Who is that? She's cute as hell." He laughed and said, "Dude, that's Kay's sister." I then replied, "Damn, I wish she went here." And, well, let's just say based on what he said next put me on a mission to go after this girl. We'll get to her later in the story. We are now finally in pads and learning plays to get ready for the jamboree. The jamboree is what they do before the actual season, and about six schools go to a football field and do quick games to just get ready for the season against other teams.

I'd say that for the first time actually playing against other teams, we did pretty well. I mean we were no 'Bama, but we definitely were building something great!

CHAPTER 2

The Guys

If I went on to explain this story without telling you about how I met all of these guys, well, I would be doing an injustice. So for that exact reason, let's start with Dalton. When I went into fourth grade, I changed elementary schools. This new elementary school was very close to my grandparents' house, so after school they would always pick me and my brother up, and we would go to their house because my parents didn't get off work till later in the day. I was over at my grandparents' a lot. Every once in a while they would ask either me or my brother to go get the mail. The reason why it was so cool to us was because the mailbox was a little ways down the road, so it was like we were big kids when we would go and get the mail. One day my Grammies (yes, I call my grandma "Grammies") asked me to go get the mail. I was so happy! I grabbed the key to the mailbox and started running down until about three-quarters of the way there I saw a kid at the mailbox. The kid's a little bit shorter than me with blond hair like a bowl on top of his head (kinda like *Dumb and Dumber*). Once I finally get close to him, I yell in my obnoxious voice, "Hiiiii!" The kid just stares at me and sprints home. The dickhead didn't even say hi back. Once I got back to the house, I went to my Grammies and said, "That kid across the street is super weird." Well, that kid across the street was Dalton, and the house was also his grandma's. That day I'll never forget because that was the day I met my best friend. Also, I'm pretty sure that situation happened before the fourth grade, but I can't remember so we're just gonna stick with it.

Next up is the one and only Brody. When I transferred to the new elementary school I didn't have any friends, and, well, to be honest, I was super lost. Finally, I met my first friend. His name was Hilton, and we hung out all the time. Over time, I became friends with his friends.

Well, Brody was Hilton's best friend. Hilton introduced me to Brody, and he and I hit it off. It wasn't until seventh grade when Hilton kinda stopped hanging with us, so we just did our own thing. Oh yeah, also Brody knew Dalton because they played baseball together, so really it was a perfect situation.

Then there's Kade. I'm gonna be honest, I have no fucking clue where he came from. I just remember for the longest time I thought he was super weird, but now he's like family to me. Love ya, Kade!

Finally, there's Jake. I knew Jake in middle school, but we didn't really hang out then. In high school, we became really good friends because we had class together and sat next to each other. You'll hear a lot more about him later on in the story.

Well, now that you know how I met all these fuckers, let me introduce them to you.

First up, we have Dalton! Dalton is a person who is pretty quiet in the beginning if you don't really know him. But let me tell ya, once you get to know him, he is one of the funniest people you'll ever meet. Also, over time, his social skills have built up a lot better to where like if we ever go anywhere as a group, he and I pretty much do all of the talking.

Next, we have Brody! So when it comes to Brody, he's not really a nervous person. But you know how some people are really honest, like almost too honest? So, that's Brody. He's a really nice guy, but he has no problem telling you how it is, which can sometimes make him look like a dick. Which, well, I mean, sometimes he is, but hey, we all are. It's tough love. Either you get it or you don't!

Now we have Kade! Kade is one of the nicest people you will ever meet, but holy shit, he's awkward! Kade will not interact with you if he doesn't know you, unless you're starting some kind of conversation, and you're most likely gonna have to carry the conversation. Once I fully knew Kade, he is hilarious, but you won't understand why it's funny unless you're in our friend group. I feel most of the time, people will look at us and think we're special, ya know? Sorry, I got off track.

Anyway, now up to bat is the man Jake. If you ever meet Jake, you'll probably just think to yourself, huh, what a nice guy that was. That's the best way to describe Jake. He is one of the nicest and most down-to-earth people I've ever met. Also, like I said, you'll hear more about him way later, so see ya later Jake!

Last but not least, yours truly, me, Hunter! Let me tell you a little about myself. I am super loud. You're probably gonna be the person in the crowd who looks at me and thinks I'm annoying. I laugh at literally everything whether it's funny or not, which can also sometimes get me in trouble. I dance all the time. And lastly, I try to be happy all the time, but sometimes it doesn't always work. But hey, you'll find that out later on in the book.

CHAPTER 3

New Beginnings

Once Zeke and I caught up with no-contact practices we could now hop into the pads and do some real practice. When hopping into the practices with the team, Dalton and Brody were still so new that when it came to certain things it was gonna take a while to build chemistry with the team. Also, I felt that some people didn't like us on the team because we literally came out of nowhere and were now starting. I mean if it was me and someone came on my turf and is now starting out of nowhere, I would be pissed. We knew all of the team captains but we didn't actually "know" them. The captain who has been going to that school forever was called Big Bird. The reason they called him this is because, well, the kid is six-foot-six, and if you don't know, six-foot-six is pretty fuckin' big. I knew all of the other captains because I used to go to school with all of them except one other whose name was Fox. But I didn't look at him as a captain because he didn't like it. He only played because Big Bird was Fox's best friend. So all of the practices were pretty good, but it didn't take much to see that we needed work and a good amount of it. At the practices, we were all making better connections with our teammates whether it be getting to know them or just fucking around with each other. The only person who just gave me a weird vibe was Big Bird. I don't know if it was because he didn't like me, he thought I was annoying, or both. I mean, don't get me wrong, we had our moments, but I just never got what it was.

Not all of the practices had them but after walk-throughs, which are the practices the day before the game, we had team dinners, which were really nice for multiple reasons. One, because we got to eat a lot sooner than usual, and two, because the food was soooo fucking good! The dinner was going really great. It was also nice that we got to spend more time with the teammates because then everyone could get to know each other better. Once I was done eating, I went to put my plate up, and one of the seniors told me no. Then one of the freshmen came by and grabbed my plate. I told him I could do it, but I guess as a freshman they pretty much have to do everything. Don't get me wrong, I get freshman duties. Everyone has to do them as a freshman, but they're not a fucking bus boy, it's not their job to clean up after you. To this day, I still disagree with it, but, hey, it's whatever. At the end of the dinner, Kay was cleaning some of the tables and I offered to help. But he said seniors don't clean the tables. So I looked at him and said, "As a senior, I'm telling you to give me the rag so that I can help you." But he still said no, so I gave it up. I never asked to help him again, but his saying no opened a door.

Later that night I did a search on Instagram to find Kay's sister. Finally, after trying to figure out which account was hers, I found her. Her account was like a beaming light coming out of my phone brighter than ever. Her name was Alyx. I've never really talked to her in person, but I definitely saw her a lot for multiple reasons, it's a super small school and she was the class president. I'll describe her more again but for now let's keep on track. Anyway, I texted her something along the lines of "Hey next time tell Kay to let me fucking help him" with a few laughing emoji. She responded and then *boom*! I was in!

We started talking a lot but just as friends. I mean, don't get me wrong, I wanted to get with her, but at the time I had a girlfriend, and although I'm a ladies' man, I'm not the type to just dump a girl and move on to the next. Well, that is until my girlfriend went batshit crazy! So Alyx and I kept talking. The night before our first game—we were playing the Elkton Elks, a pretty straightforward name—she told me that she was going to be at the game. But Kay was on the team so I wasn't shocked that she would be there, but holy shit, let me tell you, I was hyped up! I mean, it was our first game to show the people and our team what we were all about. Also, I guess a plus was the fact that Alyx was going to be there so I was trying to put on a show.

As we all got ready in the locker room, everybody was hyped, and then when the coach walked in it was all business. We all walked out in two lines just to get out on the field and start warming up. Oh man, we looked good and felt good, just warming up we were popping off on all cylinders, and I could feel that it was going to be a good day! We and Elkton are going back and forth score after score, stop after stop, finally this is when you need to have the clutch gene! If you don't know what the clutch gene is, basically it's when in game situations with all the pressure on, you come up big when it matters most. With no time on the clock, we were down and we needed the touchdown to win the game. We break out of the huddle and I snap the ball.

I'm looking all over the field and that's when I see Brody has a step on his defender, I throw the ball and it couldn't be more perfect. It lands right in his arms and *touchdown*!! We won the game. Well, at least we thought. We looked and the ref threw a flag, and they called holding on the play. Of course, everyone's saying it's a bullshit call, yada, yada, yada. We still got one more chance to score, I rolled out to the right side of the field and I threw to Big Bird, the ball was tipped and we lost the game. At this point, I still wasn't too upset because for our first game together I thought we played great, and it wasn't a league game so that helped too.

Even though it sucked that we lost, I was over it. All I had on my mind was moving on to the next game. After the game, the team hopped back onto the bus and we went and got food. The hotspot was always McDonald's, and, well, I kinda hate McDonald's now because of how much we went there. While I was waiting for my food, Big Bird was in a booth with some other people. I looked over in his direction, and the look I got back made me feel like I just disappointed my parents. I felt like this kid hated me after that game, like the whole loss was on me, even though I knew it wasn't, I sure felt like it was. Once we got done with the wonderful McDonald's, it was time to go back to the school. From there, we would go home with Dalton. Brody and I didn't have our licenses at the time so we would go everywhere with Dalton. Literally. Every day he took us home, and although he said we were annoying, I feel like sometimes he liked having us in the truck with him. There was just something about those late-night drives home that were pretty great.

Next week, we came back to school. Some people were still talking about the game but most weren't. My girlfriend and I were having problems at the time, just like any relationship. But when she got upset because I was hanging out with Brody and Dalton, that's when I called it quits. Because, well, that's family, and no one should ever get upset that you're hanging with your family. Yeah, yeah, I know. Some of you might think that's a dumb reason, but I've had enough of all the drama. Only a select few knew that I had a girlfriend, a select few meaning the whole school. But now that she was out of the picture, I was back on the market. But I didn't really want to date or go after anyone unless it was Alyx.

Alyx and I were talking all the time over text, but I never really talked to her in person because she was always busy doing student council shit. But I was pretty much just being a pussy. I'm pretty sure she knew I liked her but I still didn't know if she liked me. My first class in the morning, Alyx was in. But she was only in it to do her own work because the teacher of the class did a lot when it came to FFA, which Alyx was also in. While I was sitting at the table, one of the linemen on the team came up to me and said, "Hey man, what do you think of Alyx?" I then responded and said something like, "Well she's cute and seems cool. Why?" Even though I really liked this girl, I didn't want him to know that. He told me that she didn't have a date for homecoming and I should ask her.

Like I said, I've never really talked to her. I saw that she was working on a sign for homecoming because it said homecoming on it. I walked up to her anxiously and said, "Hey, what are you working on?" She just showed me the sign with big letters that said homecoming and laughed. I laughed with her, and then we started talking. I went back to my seat and told her I would see her later. I felt like the dumbest person in the world. I just walked up to a girl, saw exactly what she was doing, and then still repeated, "Hey, whatcha doin'?" Like, what a fucking idiot!! Even though I felt like an idiot, I was proud I walked up to her and didn't screw it up. I didn't really get nervous around people, but something about her just made me feel weird.

The one class that I was always excited for was PE. Alyx was in that class so it was, once again, a chance to get closer with her. I also had Dalton and Brody in that class, but we pretty much had every class together so it wasn't anything new. The one thing I think we were all excited for was the teacher of the class. His name was Chops. Well, at least that's what his name is gonna be in the book. Chops was one of the coolest people I've ever met. He was just an all-around down-to-earth person. We all had class with him, and we liked to flick shit toward each other, which is one reason why we were all so excited for PE. Just like any other time, I was always trying to win over Alyx, so when it came to PE I was still trying to be the main character.

Finally, after the week of school was over, it was once again time for game day! This game was huge though because it was our first home game. It was time to show all the locals how we really play football! I remember when we came out to warm up, the stands were completely empty, so the first thought I had was oh great, it's definitely gonna be a good night. As we got closer to the start of the game, there was a good amount of people who showed up. Thank God because that would suck if nobody showed up. Start of the first and they return the very first kick for a touchdown. As soon as it happened you could see the mood change on all of the teammates' faces. But the very first play, I threw it to Brody for a touchdown. When it comes to connection and a football, Brody and I are like Brady and Gronk, just not nearly as good.

We ended up winning that game, which was awesome because it was our first home game! Nobody ever told us, but once we got to the locker room, the people were talking about a fifth quarter. Fifth quarter was an after-party after all of the main home sporting events were over. They had food, drinks, games, and they were super loud, so I fit in just perfectly. Dalton, Brody, and I were all lost when we walked in, but some of the freshmen showed us how it worked and we figured it out pretty quickly. As I was looking for a spot to sit, I saw Alyx. Right when I saw her, my heart started beating faster, but it went away once we all sat down together. That whole night went by so fast. Everybody was just having such a good time that the time flew. It kinda sucked because everyone was starting to leave, and that meant I couldn't see Alyx. But right after the fifth quarter, I started texting her. We stayed up pretty late talking with each other until we were both too tired to even hold our phones. When tomorrow came, the only things I did was rest up because of the game and think about last night. I was kinda sad that it was over, but there was going to be plenty more so I didn't have any worries.

Homecoming was coming closer and closer, but nobody ever waited until the last minute to ask somebody because if you did then nobody would have time to get ready or plan anything. So, people were getting asked all over the place. I really wanted to ask Alyx but I had no clue what I was gonna do. I wanted it to be big and stand out more than everybody else's. That way, people know how I feel about her. Brody, Dalton, and I were all hanging out so we were talking about girls and if anybody was going to ask anyone, we already knew who we were going to ask. It was just figuring out how to do it. After shop class with Chops, I met Alyx at the back of the school where everybody parked their cars. She said that she needed help getting something out of her car so without hesitation I went over there. As soon as I got to her car, she threw me a little football, and my dumbass took forever to figure it out but on the back of the football in big bright orange letters it said "HOCO?" I was so happy I said, "*Hell, yeah!*" We then took pictures together, and I was shining with happiness for the rest of the day.

The girl Brody wanted to go to homecoming with, he asked her with a sign. Dalton, well, to be honest, I don't remember how he asked the girl. I just remember them going together. Knowing Dalton, he probably just looked at her and asked as simple as that! As the days went by, we were getting closer and closer to homecoming. We had a few games before the homecoming game. I'm pretty sure we lost all of them, all of them meaning one. During a practice, we were told that afterward it was Riot Night! Dalton, Brody, and I have no clue what that is, so all the kids on the team started telling us about it. So, basically, to give you the gist of it, Riot Night is when all the kids from every high school grade do different challenges or obstacle courses to see who will be the king and queen for homecoming! Every grade has a prince and a princess but there can only be one king and queen in the whole school. In the senior class, Alyx and I were nominated for prince and princess so I thought it would be cool to try and win king and queen after practice. But mostly I was just excited 'cause it was gonna be fun, especially since everybody was really competitive.

The practice started off good, but later that night it started to pour rain and it got really cold. The thing that sucked the most was that the coach ran practice too long that night so everybody was already over it. Practice finally got over and people were rushing to the locker room to get dressed for Riot Night, which was on the football field. The only thing that sucked about Riot Night was that barely any seniors came. I mean we were still winning some challenges and stuff but the other classes just overpowered us because of how many kids they had. At the end of Riot Night, they announced how many points each class had, and the class with the most points won king and queen. Out of all the classes that could have won, it was the fucking freshman. But hey, I thought it was funny that they won. Also, that night was just fun in general, so hey, no complaints from me! At the very end of Riot Night, we got together and took some group pictures and then everybody went home. It was a great night!

Now that Riot Night was over, everything was set in stone right before the homecoming game. I couldn't wait for this game for multiple reasons. One, because it was a homecoming game so a lot of people were going to be there, which meant I could try and put on a show; and two, I got to take Alyx out of a nice-ass car onto a field to take pictures. Plus, I had flowers for her, and no one else had flowers so that was pretty cool too.

So fast-forward to the homecoming game. We absolutely destroyed the other team. The final score I think was 55–14. It was awesome. I couldn't have asked for a better game and also now that the game was over that meant homecoming was up next. I was so excited for homecoming. I could list multiple reasons why I was excited but really the main reason was Alyx. Just like any dance, we all took pictures together, like a lot of pictures at multiple places too!

After all of the pictures, we all went to eat at a place called Roadhouse, basically a place that sells steaks and burgers. They sell more than that, but you're kinda weird if you don't get one of those things.

It was a super good dinner. We took some more pictures there too—shocker! Now, finally it's time for the dance, and I love dancing; well, to be honest, just music in general. Based on the song, it can change how you feel in the blink of an eye, good or bad. I think that's why I like it so much because of how strong it really is. Anyway, the dance was a great time, the most fun I've had in a long time, lots of laughs, smiles, and a ton of dancing. After the dance they were talking about a party at Fox's house. Not everyone went, but also Fox doesn't like a lot of people so it made sense to me!

I was excited because at Thurston we didn't really go to anything like this. I've never been to Fox's and some people were saying that he was rich, and, well, they weren't lying. This dude had a nice-ass house and a nice-ass pool! When I first got there, we were just kinda hanging out and talking with everybody. And then people started to get into the pool and hot tub, and so I decided to swim too. The entire night I wanted to pull a move on Alyx, and all of the guys knew it. Some were hyping me up, and others were telling me to wait. Once Fox found out, it was pretty much set in stone I was gonna pull a move. It was just about finding the confidence to do it.

I remember he told me, "Hunter, I threw this party for you so that you could kiss her, so you better do it." It just made me laugh, it never actually helped the situation. Everybody was out of the pool. Some people were in the hot tub or they were chilling by the fire so the only people in the pool were me and Alyx.

In my head, I'm thinking, finally here's your chance, *do it*! Even though I hyped myself to do it, I couldn't for some reason. It was the most nerve-racking I've ever been. So instead of pulling a move, I just talked. But just as I was about to say something, she came in and kissed me. The best way I can describe the feeling is that it's just fucking awesome! Once she did it, I didn't know what to say, but I was definitely smiling. Not everyone saw, but there were definitely a few who did see, and they could also see the big-ass smile on my face.

After we kissed, we went to the fire, talked with everybody, had a lot of laughs and good talks, and then we went home. That was homecoming night, a night that'll be hard to forget.

CHAPTER 4

A Feeling I've Never Had

On the drive home, all I could think about was Alyx. I mean, don't get me wrong, it's a good thing that I'm thinking about her 'cause clearly that means I like her a lot. But the thing that sucks is the fact that it's the only thing you're thinking about! When I tell you all the time, I mean it. Like, holy shit, you dream about her, whatever you're doing you just picture yourself being with her instead, and the craziest part about all of it was the fact we weren't even dating yet.

The next week when school came back around, everything was still the same. No feelings changed for one another and we talked like nothing happened. Deep inside, I just wanted to date this girl already. Oh yeah, a big part I left out is what happened after the homecoming party was over. We were walking together and I asked her out and she said no. Funny, right? Yeah, it wasn't; it sucked a lot.…But she had a good reason. She just wanted us to get to know each other more. So, being the great guy I am, I said, "Oh yeah, of course, no worries!" Buutttt that shit sucked. So when it came to my feelings for this girl, I was feeling more than just happy. I was also fanatical. I was scared she didn't feel the same way I did about her or if she even did like me.

So once I saw her again at school, all I was thinking about was dating her. I didn't want to rush things, though, because she wanted us to get to know each other more. You best believe I was gonna do everything in my power to make sure that happened. Instead of eating lunch with all of my other friends, we were going to her car and eating lunch. We would just talk and get to know each other like the back of our own hands. We did this all the time. After lunch, I had class with Dalton and Brody so I would tell them about all the things I learned and jokes that were said. I feel like they were annoyed sometimes, which is fair, but I told them anyway!

Personally, I would never go out of my way to try and impress someone or chase them. I'm just myself; what you see is what you get. When it came to Alyx, all I wanted to do was impress her and chase her like I'm never gonna get her. Even though we weren't dating, I had my heart set on her, and I was gonna make sure she was mine. One class where I tried so hard was PE. It was the last class of the day, and Dalton and Brody were already in it so you know it was gonna be a bomb class. And a class with sports—it was perfect!! Since Alyx was in it, I would try and act like it was a pro game or something. Plus, Chops was the teacher so the class was full of laughs too.

After the class was up, we had football practice, so before I went to the locker room to change, I would always try to find her to give her a hug or something before the day was up. It was weird, though, because even though she was on my mind all the time, once football came around, I was just in a different mindset, especially based on the day. If it was a good day, it was more of joking around and stuff at practice. If it was a bad day, then I was more serious. But let's be real, there weren't a lot of bad days.

I loved the football practices. It was just more time for football and more time with your friends to bullshit around with. I didn't do it a lot but sometimes I would talk about Alyx. All of the guys knew we were a thing, but Big Bird grew up with Alyx so she told him pretty much everything. He would tell me that she really liked me, which was perfect because, I mean, that made me feel great!

Fast-forward a little bit. We just kept going through school, and you know how it is, most days of school are all kinda the same. I just kept getting to know Alyx until finally the day came when we were gonna date. To be honest with you, I don't really remember how it happened, and I don't think it was anything special. The only thing I really know is it was a little before Halloween. The only reason I know that is because Sam, the girl Brody asked to homecoming, invited us over for a Halloween party.

Alyx and I wanted to have costumes that went hand in hand, so for the party I was Squints and she was the lifeguard from the movie *Sandlot*. The party was a lot of fun. There was just a good amount of kids from school, and I kinda liked that better than a big party anyway. I remember we were all playing cup pong but with Sprite, and Brody and I were partners, and let's just say we went on a tear and we couldn't lose! Also, the party was in a shop and they had Christmas lights hanging off of the rafters. I wanted to impress Alyx, but also it would just be fun. So, there was a baseball bat, and, well, since I was Squints, why not?! Brody and I started pitching each other's Sprite cans and hitting them with the bat. It was fun, but I wanted to hit a dinger, and about that time Brody pitched me one right down the middle and *boom*! It's a *homer*!! Right into the light. I blew one of the bulbs up with the Sprite can. It was funny, but at the same time I also felt like an idiot. But Alyx laughed so it must have worked.

After being in the shop for a little while, everybody decided to go into the house to watch a movie. Nobody actually watched a movie. We mostly went upstairs to a living room and everybody visited. I was happy though because that meant more time with Alyx. I just kept learning more about her, whether it be the thing that makes her smile, all the way to the food she hates, or things she liked as a kid. I was learning everything about her, and I loved every second of it. It started to get late so Dalton, Brody, and I had to go. I just gave her a hug and said bye, and of course, on the car ride home, all I can think about is Alyx! As time went on, we just started hanging out more and more. She met my parents, and I already knew her parents 'cause of football, but I met her grandparents and everything else. Then we started to get closer and closer until one day those three big words were said—I Love You. I don't know who said it first. I just remember the feeling I had when they were said and it was fucking nuts!

Also, as you start to say these things, your feelings are pretty crazy for each other. So, just like any other teenager, you find an empty parking lot or something else and you just go nuts on each other! I'm just talking like making out, nothing more. And oh man, I've never really done that before, and holy shit, I don't know how to describe it. But to keep it PG on my part, you know how Jordan Belfort describes Naomi in *The Wolf of Wall Street*? Well, basically something like that, just a little less, ya know, bad. But anyway, you get it, we are really crazy about each other.

The reason I called this chapter "A Feeling I've Never Had" is because this feeling is like no other. This is a feeling that is great and awful in its own way all at the same time, and when you're younger, I feel like it's a lot worse. For instance, the reason why the feeling of love is like this is because while you're feeling like you're on top of the world and you have no worries, at the same time you're also sad 'cause you're not with them right now. Plus, you're also curious if you're overthinking everything in the world because you want to make sure they feel the exact same thing.

Also, though this is just some of my experience with it, if anyone told you there was a certain definition for love, they're full of shit. There are so many different ways to define love, it's absolutely crazy. I love a lot of people, and when I say that word, it means different things for different people. Like I love my friends, but I wouldn't want to kiss my friends 'cause that's fucking weird. But when you say it to a girl, it's a little different. Like you want to do everything in the world with them and not worry about anything and kiss them!

Also, the reason I say love is harder for younger people is because I feel like they don't actually understand it. When it comes to adults, they will do anything and everything for the person they love. But as a kid in high school or just a young person, they don't understand that. I don't blame young people for not understanding it. I mean, let's be real. As a kid who's nineteen or twenty-one years old, I wouldn't want to get married or tied down or whatever you wanna call it, because you're young and deep down you know all good things must end. And yeah, you might have the same friends and stuff as you did growing up, but you're never gonna be able to do what you did when you were kids.

I believe in young love, and there are a lot of kids who want that, and if they get it, then more power to them. Just personally, I feel like a lot of young people are confused when it comes to love, and for that reason, they just do their own thing until one day it comes to them. But I can tell you this, when it came to Alyx, I wasn't thinking like one of those younger kids that didn't understand it.

CHAPTER 5

The Last Game

I can't remember the exact number of football games we played, but I wanna say it was like nine or something. We weren't going to make the playoffs or anything because our record was no bueno, but we had a lot of good games and some shit games. Although some people would look at the game and be like, "Well, if you aren't going to the playoffs what's the point?" Well, you see the point of this game is just respect and ending the season on a win. Coming into this game, that's the one thing that mattered the most to me—ending my high school football career on a win.

Every single game we played, I always came in with confidence. I was confident about this game too but something just felt different. I don't know if it was because it was my last high school game or if it was something else, but it just felt like a big deal. Everybody was warming up and getting ready for the game and you could tell everybody was ready. One thing that made me hyped for the game was that Dalton was starting. He started a few other games before this one, but in particular I was more excited for this one.

Also, I'm not gonna lie to you. Dalton is probably the slowest receiver you'll ever see, yet he will get open every play. I don't understand how, and when he is open, it's like the dude has glue on his hands. He will not drop a pass. He's the most deceiving receiver ever.

Anyway, it was finally time for the game and we were starting with the ball. It was our first drive and we were killing them. They couldn't stop us until the one play came up that changed the whole momentum of the game. It was an end around, but instead of me being under center I was in shotgun. The concept of an end around is to make the defense think you're throwing the ball. So you call the receiver in motion and right before he passes, you hike the ball and toss it to him. This is exactly what I did, and oh man, it was gonna work like a charm. But the receiver dropped the ball, and it was behind the line of scrimmage so it was a fumble. The defense picked the ball up and ran it all the way back to score a touchdown.

If I told you the momentum changed, that would be an understatement. After that touchdown, we couldn't get anything going. We were stuck in a hole that we couldn't get out of. We would have a few big plays but they never went anywhere. And to add to everything, they were double-teaming Brody so he couldn't get open. So you may ask, "Well, who was the main receiver that game?" His name is Dalton Martin, a.k.a. Mullet Man, a.k.a. Cap D, a.k.a.... well, you get it.

Like I was saying, Dalton wasn't very fast yet he still got open. There were some plays where he caught the ball in this game, but the main one was a flag route. I threw it over the top of his right shoulder and the play went for about thirty yards until the ball got stripped and they scored again. Before Dalton got up, I saw him punch the ground with aggression after the play was over. On the inside, I wanted to make fun of him but that would not help a thing. Instead, I told him it was OK and that we'll get it next play.

After that play, we got back into the huddle and did more and more plays that led to nothing. Later on in the game, Brody scored a touchdown and it wasn't a pretty job by me. Not a single thing was going our way and we knew it. But that wasn't going to stop us from playing our hearts out. I can't remember the score but I know it was a lot to a little and they won. It was definitely a bummer to end your high school football career in a loss, but hey, no one can say we didn't try.

After the game, we of course shook the opposing team's hands and said good game just like you do every other game, and then everybody scattered across the field talking to different friends and family members. I was one of the last ones to the locker room because I took some pics with Alyx and was talking with my family and her family. I was a little emotional, but I wasn't crying mostly because I just didn't want anybody to see it. Brody was still on the field, and he was squatted down looking all around.

I was done talking with everyone and I went over to him to give him a hug, and that's when I heard a sniffle. I kinda just bit on my tongue and wasn't gonna cry until I saw him and the sadness in his eyes. I've seen a lot of people sad in my life and for different reasons, but I've never seen the look that he had. He looked as if he was the most lost person in the world, and as soon as I saw him, I couldn't hold back my tears. They fell from my face so effortlessly I didn't even have to try and cry. It just happened, and there was nothing I could do.

I just lost one of the things I loved the most in the world and there was nothing I could do about it. I couldn't go back to play one more snap. I couldn't play another game because there wasn't one. This was the last one. See there was also a very big difference between me and Brody growing up. I always watched football with my dad, having fantasies of how I was gonna play with Adrian Peterson one day and win a Super Bowl and stuff like that. But I didn't play when I was a kid because my parents couldn't afford it. But, you see, Brody had the same dreams, but that kid was born into football. He's been playing ever since he was a little kid, so when I talk about seeing him and crying, I could only imagine what Brody was actually feeling inside.

I remember trying to make jokes to lighten the mood up, but that shit did not work. We were both way too sad. Finally, we got to the locker room and I was pretty much done crying. I sat down and started to take off my cleats, and then I saw Big Bird crying and Brody crying and everyone just sad, some a lot more than others. Then I started to think about growing up and playing football with the guys during recess and in the backyard and the whole nine yards. And then I couldn't stop crying. The waterworks were happening and now they were a full go.

Growing up, most people say it's just a game, and this doesn't go for just football, this goes for every sport anybody plays. I know every single person has heard that at least once in their life, and that's OK because you know it's so much more than that. See, since it was my last game, I knew I was gonna miss it, but really I feel it just makes you think about things more than anything. It makes you think about growing up and playing with your friends and all the teammates I've had and the relationships I've built with them and the impact they've had on my life and the impact I've had on theirs. Once you think about all of those things, that's the real tearjerker. You realize you just lost one of your families that you won't ever play with again. That's why the last game was the game I will always remember.

CHAPTER 6

The Next Season

After football season, we didn't really have much off time until basketball season started up. I'd say we had about two weeks and then basketball practice started up. I was in good shape, but there is a big difference between football shape and basketball shape so the first couple practices kinda killed me. But once I got into the groove, it was all good.

I loved basketball almost as much as football, but the thing with basketball is I grew up playing it. I'm the kid in basketball who is probably the most bipolar player ever. Either I have a great game or you need to get me off the court because I'm straight garbage. Out of Dalton, Brody, and me, Dalton is by far the best basketball player. He has a really weird jump shot, but hey, so did Larry Bird and look at how good he was.

We had a lot of practice before we actually got into the regular season but we also had nonleague games, basically preseason games. The practices were becoming better and better as we were learning more plays and learning how each person plays on the team. It started inching closer to the first nonleague game of the season but no one cared. To us, it was the first game of the season, and because of that coach was gonna put the lineup on the whiteboard for our first game. Everyone wanted to know what the lineup was because that tells you who the starters are and who wasn't going to start that game?

Finally it was posted, and well, let's just say I was disappointed. Neither Dalton, nor Brody, nor I was starting. To be honest, I was shocked because I thought that at least one of us would have started, but shit, I guess not. Anyway, the first game, it's finally here! Everybody is so pumped, and since everybody was that way, we were all just feeding off of each other's energy. One thing that was cool was that most of the games we played, the girls also played the same school's girls team, so we took one bus together with all the players. This was cool because it's a bigger group. Alyx played basketball so I got to see her even more. She was good. She was the PG (point guard) so I cheered her on whenever we watched their games.

During football, the bus rides were one of my favorite things. I could tell based on the first bus ride that I was gonna love the bus rides and it all had to do with one JBL speaker. I know what I just said might sound crazy, but you have no clue how important that speaker was. You may be thinking, "Well, who brought the speaker?" Well, you already know—the one and only Big Bird brought it every bus ride. Later, I will explain more about how the speaker had such a big impact, but for now, I'll just say mood-changer.

After about a three-hour bus ride, we finally made it to the school we were gonna be playing at. It was some kind of charter school in a place I'd never heard of. First up were the girls, and if I remember right, I think they completely destroyed the other team like it wasn't even a competition for them. We played next and we were hyped up, of course. But you could tell people had the jitters, but once the tip happened, they were gone. The guy who started instead of me was pretty good, but he was younger than me so it pissed me off that he was starting. But after about the first quarter, that's when Dalton and I both went in. Brody would soon follow, or maybe he went in before us. Shit, I don't remember. All I know is once we went in things started clicking better.

Also, I think one reason it flowed better was because everyone who was in the starting lineup played football except for one person. So even though it was a different sport, we kinda knew everyone's playing style. In football, I couldn't really connect with Big Bird. But oh man, this was different. It's like we had perfect chemistry on the court! When it came to Dalton and Brody, well, we grew up playing together so we already had that spark. And when it came to everyone else, we were learning how to play with each other but we were learning fast.

The team we were playing against wasn't very good but it had one kid who was cooking the whole team. This kid literally had the build of a basketball player and moved and walked like one. But his weakness was he didn't have a consistent shot. He would knock them down every once in a while, but I mean, everybody does that. Where he really killed you was inside. If he drove to the paint, it was a guaranteed bucket or foul. We couldn't stop him, so instead of stopping him we made a plan to slow him down. Some of the other kids could ball, but they weren't anything special. Get in their face, put a hand up, and then they pretty much stopped.

I can't remember what the score was, but it was a really good game and we came out with the win! This was the best because the girls and boys both won! The bus ride home was like a party with people laughing, dancing, singing, and anything else you can think of. Plus, I got more time to hang with Alyx! After the game, we stopped somewhere to eat, and listen, I have nothing against McDonald's because, I mean, like if you need cheap food, it is right there for you. But holy shit, I was burned out on Mickey D's. We would eat there after almost every football game, so the fact we were gonna repeat it during basketball season kinda sucked. But hey, still good times because this was also a time to bullshit with people more and kinda learn who they were.

Every day was kinda becoming the same, it was all planned out. Go to school, eat lunch with Alyx, go hard in PE, and then basketball practice. Rinse and repeat, but I loved every day. Now that the season started, we were starting to have games a lot more. League games were starting, which were the important games. The girls were also in the same league so we always played the same schools, which was pretty nice. So, after a few practices, we finally made it to our first league game. It was away but only about an hour, maybe an hour and a half at max. When we first walked into their gym, I was shocked. It was a pretty small gym, like the out-of-bounds line was about a shoe length away from the bleachers, so not much room to inbound the ball. Anyway, the girls always played first and it was a massacre. The game wasn't even fair, it's almost like the girls on the other team didn't know how to play basketball. Next up was us. We came out and started doing warm-ups. Then, we saw their team. They had brothers in the starting lineup, and they were both pretty tall guys. And they had some really short players, but damn, they will cross you up. Basically, the team was pretty good, but we were better and everyone knew it.

Tip starts and it's instantly physical and fast-paced. I was guarding one of the brothers. The one I was guarding kinda looked like a cracked-out Klay Thompson, but he definitely didn't play like Klay. This guy was very physical and kind of a dirty player. Once he got the ball, he would just back down and he either shot the fade or passed out. But every time he would back down, he always threw an elbow at you, and it was the most annoying fucking thing in the world. It just made you wanna throw the basketball at his face, but I didn't. All you could do was play ball. The scoring was going back and forth. Nobody was really pulling away, but I think right before halftime, they got a pretty good lead, and we were down by about nine. In the locker room, everyone was pretty pissed. We were playing sloppy basketball and now our heads are making it worse for ourselves. Everyone just needed to take some breaths and focus before we got back out there because if we went out there before we got out of our heads, we were gonna get crushed.

Second half we started off a little slow, they weren't pulling away anymore and it was just staying about the same. I'd say about the middle of the third quarter was when we started clicking. We were hitting all cylinders, and we just needed to keep at that speed. We came back and we had a little lead. We weren't pulling away, and it kept going back and forth again. Now we're in the fourth and the game is really close. I can't remember the time it happened, but it was close to the end of the game. Someone on their team threw a pass and I jumped it. I was sprinting to the hoop to score. I knew someone was behind me so I jumped up for the layup, and as I jumped, I got tackled in midair. As soon as I hit the ground, I screamed. I landed right on my thumb, and oh man, that shit hurt. I couldn't even catch the ball. I shot my free throws with one hand because it hurt to touch the ball with my left hand. I somehow made both of them and then sat my happy ass on the bench and cheered the team on!

We ended up pulling away and winning our first league game of the season! Everybody was super hyped, as they should be. The only problem was my thumb was the size of a balloon. Alyx got me some ice to put on my thumb, and let's just say the bus ride back was very long. I didn't really want to go to the doctor, but the swelling was not going down, so I went and got X-rays. I split the top of my thumb in half. It wasn't the biggest break in the world, but the doctor told me I shouldn't play anymore and wait for it to heal. There was no way in hell I was doing that, so I just got a splint and then during practice I would wrap it up. There were certain times if someone passed me the ball hard, it would hurt so bad, but I kinda got used to it. But holy shit, I didn't think I could get worse at basketball, but after I broke my thumb, my whole form and everything was gone.

I would love to go on and tell you about every game we played during the season, but I'm not trying to write the most boring book in the world. Instead, we'll just skip ahead to the playoffs. Yeah, we made the playoffs, and it was pretty badass. The first game we had coming up was against The Falls. We watched film on them, but in all the film we saw they didn't look like the best team. So, to be honest, I think we all kinda walked into this game thinking it wouldn't be that hard and the practices were not going the best. But when it came to game time, we were ready! The game started off pretty fast but nothing crazy. I just remember no one was really pulling away until the fourth quarter. See, everybody has that one game of their life where they are just unstoppable, and when I say unstoppable, I mean you can't do anything. Your defense could be the best in the world and it doesn't even matter. The point guard on The Falls was having that game! This kid was single-handedly fucking our team, and we couldn't do anything about it! I mean every single shot this kid was taking was going in. You know how in *2K*, you'll turn the sliders all the way up so that you'll make everything? Well, yeah, this kid had the sliders all the way up! I liked our point guard. He was pretty good, but he was a ball hog. Usually, I would be pissed that he wasn't passing, but our point guard was also having the game of his life.

It was our first playoff game and it was literally a battle between two people. There was very little time on the clock, and they were up, and neither of us was slowing down. Finally, they started double-teaming our point guard, so he passed out and then *bang*! A corner three, nothing but net, and guess who made it? The one, the only, Dalton-fucking-Martin! Now they were screwed 'cause Dalton started to catch fire. In the fourth, I think Dalton made like three or four threes, and we ended up winning. Everyone was so hyped 'cause we were one step closer to Baker, and Baker was state, which is exactly where we wanted to go!

Next week, we found out that we played Trinity next, and they were a high-seeded team. They were this private school that was like three hours away, and of course, we had to travel. We definitely took this game a lot more seriously, especially because this was the game that would send us to Baker if we won. Most of the practices were going well and nobody had doubts about the game. We were all walking tall with a lot of confidence. Some of the girls from the basketball team rode on the bus with us because they wanted to come and watch the game. Like I was saying, after I broke my thumb, my form was all off, and I never really got it back for the rest of the season. Before warm-ups, we were all shooting around, and while I was shooting, Alyx told me I should try tucking my arm in more on my shot. So I tried it, and after I did it, I'd never shot better in my life. My form was finally back, and it was right before the most important game of my life. I was making everything in warm-ups. I couldn't miss!

Finally, it was game time. Everybody had their assignment on who to guard and it was perfect. Everybody was actually doing a great job! We were sticking with this team that was a top-five-seeded team, and I think they were shocked. In the first quarter, I had twelve points and shot five for seven, and those were the only points I had for the rest of the game. Going into the second quarter we were only down by six but for some reason our point guard wanted to switch up who was guarding who. Somehow, I ended up guarding the six-foot-six point guard on Trinity. Why the fuck would I ever guard a point guard when I play power forward? Also, why would our coach just be OK with this happening? Going into halftime I think we were probably down by like twenty. During halftime, we had some talk about how we gotta be quicker on defense, but nobody was in a good mood because of how the game was going and the fact that it seemed like our coach didn't give a shit. After the half, all of us seemed like we were ready to play but it was just all downhill. The ball hog was hogging, and the team was falling apart. Some of us were still working together, but if everyone's not in it, then it doesn't matter. We ended up losing the game and that was the end of our season. Just like that, it was over! A pretty shitty way for the season to end, but hey, nothing we could do about it anymore. On the bus ride back, there was a lot of talking about oh, if this happened or that happened, but to be honest, some kids looked happy that the season was over. To be honest, I think a lot of them looked happy because of all the bus riding, and a lot of them either didn't play or they didn't like some of the players.

But hey, that was the last time I would ever play basketball in high school, so, I mean, it definitely sucked. But it didn't hit me hard like football did. It just kinda gave me a sad feeling when I thought about it because, I mean, once again, it's another sport that I'll never play again in school.

CHAPTER 7

Worldwide Scare

After our loss to Trinity, the girls team still had a game to see if they could go to Baker and they ended up winning! Which was great for them. I think they ended up losing in either the first or second round, but, I mean, hey, they went, so that's pretty cool.

Once both of our seasons ended, there was a break before any more sports happened, and I'm not gonna lie to you, I was pretty happy about it. Although I love sports, they can take a big toll. I mean, it takes up a lot of your time, and it can be mentally and physically draining. So it was kinda nice to have a break.

See, the only thing that kinda sucks about nothing going on besides school is there isn't really anything to look forward to. It was almost like you were just stuck in the same day over and over again. Of course, there were different things in the day that would make certain days better than others, but there was nothing drastic.

As school went on, we were preparing more and more for finals. In one of my classes, we were starting to learn about different laws, court cases, the best ways to fight the cases, how people either won or lost the case, and different tactics they would use in court. It was pretty interesting and I really enjoyed it. The cool thing about the class, though, is that Dalton, Brody, and Alyx were in it.

One day we came into class and our teacher straight-up handed us books and called it a worksheet. I'm not sure what everyone else was thinking, but I was freaking out because she just threw this on us out of nowhere. Everyone took their seats and that's when she then announced the assignment. The assignment was a court case that we had to figure out. The whole class had the same case, but we weren't supposed to solve the case with the class. Instead, you got to pick your own team and everyone had a role on your team, and you would integrate the other teams you were going against. Then each team would get graded on how well it did.

As she's telling us the directions, Dalton, Brody, and I all look at each other. We already knew we were gonna be on a team, and if you put the three biggest smart-asses in the world on a team in a court case, it's bound for greatness! While this huge assignment was going on, we also had AP economics to worry about. (Note to readers: Before I go any further, I just wanna say I don't have a clue why the fuck I would ever do AP economics. That shit is so hard. But anyway, back to the story!)

In AP econ, I also had Dalton, Brody, and Alyx in the class 'cause, you know, it's a super small school so there weren't many options. Most of the time—and when I say most of the time, I mean like 85 percent of the time—I was lost. I literally had no clue what the fuck the teacher was talking about. And then when I would look lost, he would call on me to answer a question. And guess what? I would get it wrong. It wasn't just me he did it too, though. I mean he did it to everyone in class. Just the other people kinda knew what they were talking about, and I didn't know what I was talking about.

We had this class every day, and right after was the class with the court case. That class was right next door to AP econ. One day, Alyx and I went to her house for "lunch." The reason why it's "lunch" and not lunch is because if we went to her house we weren't eating, we were just gonna make out the whole time, which, I mean, as a teenage boy, I didn't have a problem with. Alyx had this great idea that we should just skip econ because there wasn't anything important going on that day. I've never skipped class in my life, and if we were both gone and came back to the next class, it would be pretty obvious we skipped class together. But at this point, I wasn't thinking straight so I said, "Uhh, fuck yeah!" One other huge problem with this is that Dalton and Brody knew I was with Alyx, and when they knew something that was kinda embarrassing, they were brutal and they would call you out forever! After econ was done, Alyx and I were there for the next class and we saw the econ teacher. He kinda made a comment because I'm pretty sure he knew what was going on, especially since Alyx's face was as red as a tomato! *Ohh,* and then came Dalton and Brody, and, no shit, I probably heard them joke about it that day fifty times, and I heard about it for the next month!

School still pretty much stayed the same. The only two classes that were hard were AP econ and the class with the court cases. The one thing that made school a little cooler was the fact that prom was getting close. See, to most people, they would look at prom as just a dance. But to me, it was the last dance I would ever have in my life. Growing up, I would see all of those high school movies where they talk about their lives and how after school, life's not gonna be the same so they have to make it a night remember. I loved those movies, so as soon as I heard prom was close, I was getting hyped. Alyx and I were already talking about what kinda things we were gonna wear, who's gonna throw the after-party, where to eat, and yada, yada, yada. I wanted prom to be exactly like the movies, so my head was filled with ideas!

Anyway, like I was saying, besides prom, school was just the same shit but a different day—until one day in econ. So, earlier in the year, there was a talk about this new virus and how it's gonna kill a shit ton of people, and it's like crazy strong, and it's called the coronavirus. Well, when people first heard about it, there were a bunch of memes about it because, well, it's called corona, so people instantly thought about alcohol. But they were also comparing it to Ebola, and everybody laughs about that because, well, to be honest, I don't know why people joked about Ebola, but anyway, they did. Well, I actually took notice when it hit France. I'm not much of a news watcher but I saw it was all over, and that thousands of people were dying daily in France. There were so many bodies that they couldn't take care of them or something along those lines.

So anyway, we went to school like any normal day, but there were rumors that we might miss some school. Of course, when we heard that, we all kinda laughed like "Ohh, OK! Not gonna happen!" That is until we walked into economics. The teacher said before we started class that he wanted to talk about something important. Well, that important thing was corona. He then went on to tell us something like: "Hey everybody, so it's not a for-sure thing yet, but we are preparing to miss a couple weeks of school because of the coronavirus. We will be issuing everybody a Chromebook unless you have some kind of computer at home to do schoolwork on." As soon as he said this, everybody started asking questions about the virus, how serious it actually was, and how school was going to keep going. Of course, he didn't know—I mean, shit, nobody knew—what was going to happen.

After econ, no class was really the same because everybody just kept talking about what was going to happen. After the court case class, we had PE, buuttt I don't think we ended up making it to PE. In class, that is when they announced that the day was over. Everybody had to sign this sheet to take a Chromebook, and based on where you signed, that was the number you were assigned. After everybody was assigned their Chromebooks, they then went on to tell us the game plan for what was going to happen. We were going to miss two weeks of school, and we would have different assignments we would have to complete and turn in through this thing called Google Classroom online until we came back to school. Once we heard the game plan, we were all hyped! Two weeks out of school and we have to do a few assignments online and turn them in? I mean, like, dude, what a fucking cakewalk! The next two weeks were pretty great. The boys and I would hang out, play video games, and really just kinda enjoy life without school for a little bit! The only thing that sucked is that I couldn't see Alyx because her parents were pretty stressed about the whole thing.

The two weeks ended up going by pretty fast, and all of us were pretty excited to get back and see all of our friends again. The only problem was we couldn't go back yet. I guess the schools still weren't ready to open up because corona was just getting worse. So now instead of just doing some assignments online, we had full-on school through a computer. They set everybody up with a thing called Zoom, which is just an online video chatting app. So, every morning I would wake up and go to my computer to stare at my teacher and some kids through a screen and try my best to learn something even through the shitty connection. For the first couple days, I took it pretty seriously, but after that, I didn't really give a shit. Dalton, Brody, and I would go into a class, mute our mics, turn our cameras off, and play video games while the teacher was teaching. See, usually I would listen, but the problem was because all the classes were online, they had to completely change some of the shit we were learning in the beginning to things that were easier to explain over a computer.

See, now I don't know what everyone else was thinking, but when I tell you the days were long, I mean it. I've never been more dead in my life. I started to lose motivation to really do anything other than stare at a screen all day. The one nice thing was that Alyx's parents started to kinda chill about everything going on so we would hang out when we could. I would love to tell you that after just a few more weeks we went back to school and life was amazing, but if I told you that I would be the biggest liar in the world. Here's what really happened. After a few more weeks of school, they announced that we were gonna be doing this online school bullshit for the rest of the year! So, life just continued to be hell. Every day, stuck in your house doing school through a computer and not being able to go back to see your friends. At this point, I don't think anybody was used to it, but we knew that nothing was going to change, so we just accepted the fact that this was how it was going to be.

The year was very weird because out of nowhere, it started to fly by fast. What I mean by that is that it was already time to start figuring out colleges and all of that shit. Yes, I know that you do that throughout the year, but I didn't do it yet and the deadline was coming fast. When it came to applying and working on an essay to send to a college, I didn't have a clue where to start and I needed help. Thankfully, Dalton also didn't know what he was doing, so we were both lost together.

Even though we weren't going to school anymore, we were still very close to Chops. We told him that we needed help, and like the GOAT he is, he helped us out! Dalton and I went to the school pretty early, I'd say probably 10:00. Once we got there, we went over the colleges we wanted to apply to and the requirements it takes to get into them. We probably spent the whole day there, and then the next day, we came back to finish up all of the work. Chop's wife, Kat, took the time to review and edit my essay so I could send it to a college.

The thing that made my essay a little different from most is I didn't have anything to back it up. See, when you send in your transcripts or your essay or whatever it may be, they can usually see clear as day that you have the grades or the community service or whatever it is you need, but I didn't have any of that. My freshman and sophomore years, I dealt with anxiety and depression super bad, to the point that I would make myself sick just so that I didn't have to go to school. I missed months and months of school, which was setting me up for failure more than I knew. Going into my junior year, I wasn't even close to being on track to graduate, so I set up a meeting with my student counselor to ask her what I could do.

She told me there was this class I could take online that was just a bunch of different classes in one to basically test your knowledge on different subjects, and if you passed a subject, then you would get a credit. You need twenty-four credits to graduate, so at the bare minimum, six credits a year. The best thing about this class was that you could work at your own pace because everyone in the class was doing something different. I didn't want anything more than to just be back on track. I can't quite remember but I finished my junior year with about fifteen credits, which put me on track and a little bit more! OK, so now that we're all caught up, back to it!

So, since I didn't have the cumulative GPA for really any college, I had to back it up with what I knew best—talking! I could talk up a storm to anyone, so that's exactly what I did in the essay. I explained everything I'd been through, how there's not gonna be a more hard-working kid than me, and that I wouldn't let them down—the whole nine yards! After Dalton and I reviewed all of our shit, we sent it through, or I should say Chops sent it through. It was one of the nicest things anyone's done for me, and it's something I'll never forget. Chops, Dalton, and I went and got some lunch at Burrito Amigos after everything was done. We all just kinda visited and talked about all the crazy shit going on in the world. It was super nice to not have to worry about anything anymore and just relax, so lunch was really great!

Since everything was sent in, all we could do now was wait to see if we got in. Online school kept going on but during online class, all of the seniors had to join one video chat. In the video chat they told us that we were done with school, we didn't even have to do a senior project. That was it. School was done. I think we were done three months before anybody else. Of course, we didn't have diplomas or anything yet. We were still planning all of that out. But school was not a thing anymore.

Well, since school wasn't around, I had to get a job. Of course, the job was only gonna be temporary until college started up, but I needed something to start building money. I didn't really know what kinda job I wanted, but Kade just got a job at KFC, and working with a close friend would be pretty cool. He said I could get hired pretty easily because they needed people. So, I said fuck it and applied there. I got a call from them later in the day and went in for an interview the same day. I got the job like it was nothing. The interview wasn't even an interview, so I was happy about it!

During the interview, I told them I needed a couple days off because graduation was in a couple weeks. Once they said yes, I accepted the job! My first day and really my first couple weeks were all just training. They had me working as a cashier or I would help prep food. Kade was the cook so I didn't really see him much. But if we ever did see each other, we were just as dumb to each other as we usually were, which made the job really fun sometimes. Graduation came really fast, which was super cool and really shitty all at the same time. Because of COVID, we couldn't have a normal graduation so we set up a graduation through cars and trucks. Well, we didn't, but the amazing teachers did.

So, everybody met at this church in the neighborhood, and then from there it was a big parade for all of the kids graduating. I can't remember the order it was in, but I know my family drove in front of Dalton's and Dalton's drove in front of Brody's, which was super cool because we got to stay close together during graduation instead of one person at the front of the line and the others at the end. Everybody was driving in a line toward the high school and there were drones flying above us so if different families couldn't make it, they were live streaming it on YouTube. Once we got to a certain point at the school, we split into three different lines of cars. Shockingly, it was actually pretty organized, and of course, the boys were next to each other in line. There was a photographer there for the *Register-Guard*, and as we were pulling in, Dalton and I reached over the beds of our trucks and locked our hands together. As we did, he took a picture, and we were hoping to make it in the newspaper. Before people got out of their trucks to get their diploma, there were speeches from the valedictorian, who was Alyx, and the teacher voted by the students to give a speech who was, of course, Chops. I can't really remember the speeches, but I remember I clenched my jaw during Chop's speech because as he was giving the speech, I started thinking about all the times in school. The speeches were finally done, and now it was time to go up and get our diplomas. As you got your diploma, you couldn't shake anybody's hand. Instead, your diploma was set up on a podium where you would grab it, take a picture, and then hop back in the truck.

After I hopped back in the bed of the truck, we headed back to the church where everybody was going to take pictures or something else. I remember once we got there, I gave Chops this card basically telling him thank you for everything that you've done, and he's not much of a hugger but I think I got one after he read it. After that, we took pictures with everyone, and then we headed home. Everybody had some kind of graduation party afterward so I talked with Dalton and Brody and we were going to hang out the next day or something. Alyx wasn't having a party till later so she was gonna come over to my place. At my house, it was really nice. I got to see and visit with a lot of family, have a lot of laughs, and eat some food because I was so hungry! Once Alyx got to my house, she started visiting with everybody, and she brought Kay and the rest of her family, so her family started visiting with mine, and we started to play ping-pong and just kinda hang out.

After a little while, people started to head home, and then the only people that were at my house were my family, Alyx, and Kay. I can't remember but my family ended up leaving and so Alyx, Kay, and I watched a movie. Once the movie was over, they headed out and then it was just me in the house alone. This sucked. I didn't cry or anything, but I remember that night I just kinda sat in silence thinking about how life goes by so fast and how I never listened to my parents when they said it goes by fast. Then the memories of growing up with all of my friends and how we were not kids anymore started coming in, and that's when my eyes watered up a little bit. That whole night I didn't stop thinking once about how school was finally over and how we had to go into the real world.

Remember how I was saying I sent my college stuff in at the last minute? Because of that, it took a little longer, and then COVID doubled the time it normally would take so it was a really long wait. But after waiting for so long, I finally got a letter in the mail! As soon as I got the mail, I ripped it open, and inside was a letter that said, "Thank you for your application, but at the time you don't meet our school's requirements," or something along the lines of that. You see, I don't really know why but I didn't want to go to a community college even though it was my last option. The idea of going to a community college killed me! The dumbest thing about it too was the fact that it was way cheaper and Dalton was going, so why the fuck not go! I can get into the whole situation more later in the book, but anyway, I ended up not going. Instead, I told myself I was gonna work and find out what I want to do for the rest of my life that way. My dad worked as a sterile processor at a hospital. If you don't know what that is, basically they clean all the instruments and get them ready for the doctors before surgeries. He told me that the hospital was hiring housekeepers and that it would be a great opportunity to get my foot in the door if I wanted to go further in the medical field. The job paid a lot more than KFC, and I love people, so who knows, maybe trying to be a nurse would be cool! I applied for the job, went in for an interview, and a couple days later I got a call asking if I wanted the job.

See, I grew up around the hospital because when I was younger my Grammies used to work there so I knew about 75 percent of the housekeepers already. I kinda had an in because I knew the boss. But hey, that's beside the point, I got the job! When it comes to jobs, the hospital is definitely a lot more complicated. Also, the hospital is union so as soon as you get hired, there's a good amount of meetings you have to go to and a lot of paperwork. My first day was orientation, which I thought was going to be with the other housekeepers that were just hired, but it was also new nurses, security guards, scrub techs, etc. I was already sticking out like a sore thumb because everyone was dressed business casual and I was wearing white Vans with rolled-up blue Levi's and a Kevin Durant SuperSonics shirt. I guess there was an email that went out telling you what to wear, but clearly I didn't get the memo, and the person running our orientation made sure it didn't go unnoticed.

By looking at a person, you can usually read them, and, well, these people were easy to read! Half of them were there for a paycheck and then they were gone, and others were there to start drama and gossip with other people. I learned that half of the hospital was all drama and gossip anyway, which is kinda crazy, but I guess that's just the way things roll! After the orientation and all the other meetings, I finally had my first real day. I was starting my training with a woman by the name of Byrdie. The name sounded familiar, and then it finally clicked. Growing up, she was the second highest up to my Grammies and that's how I remembered her. She was a really nice lady. It took her just a little bit to remember me. On my second day, she asked if I was Les's kid, and once I said yes, you could see her face kinda spark up and then she remembered. My training was pretty easy because as a housekeeper you just do a lot of cleaning. But there are certain ways to clean everything, and certain rooms would be different from others because of the illness that a patient had. For that reason, there was a lot of training and a lot of tests.

When it came to me as a person, I was a night owl. I fucking loved it! I mean, I would rather hold something out and do it at night because I thought the night was just better. Well, for that reason, I worked the swing shift, which meant I could stay up all night because I didn't go to work until 3:00 and I didn't get off until 11:30. The only thing that sucked with the shift was the schedule. It was always four-on, two-off, which means your days off are changing all the time and you never truly had a set schedule. Since I worked during the night, Alyx and I would either hang out on my days off or we would hang out before I went to work. The guys and I would hang out after I got off because all of us stayed up late, so it worked out. We were all playing video games one night, and we started talking about getting our own place so we could just hang out whenever we want and be as loud as we wanted without any parents getting pissed off. While all of us were talking about this, Kade's basement was brought up. Kade's basement used to be a day care back in the day run by his mom and his stepdad. I guess it was a pretty nice place! The basement was not a nice place anymore; it was basically a storage unit for shit that nobody needs and garbage.

The nice thing about the basement was that Brandon (Kade's stepdad) wanted the shithole cleaned anyway. So, we offered him a deal—all of us would clean up the basement, make dump runs, and pay for it all but only if we could use it as our own man cave. Brandon said he didn't give a shit what we did if we were gonna clean the place up; the basement was all ours! Once he said those magic words, that's when the work started. We tried to work around everybody's schedule so we could clean it together. It definitely took a lot of scrubbing and hard work, but I think after about a week we had it all cleaned up and it was ready for furniture and stuff to go in. Everybody had a different idea of what they wanted in the basement and how the furniture was going to be placed. But the one thing that all of us wanted was a big mounted TV. Brandon knew we wanted a TV for the basement, and since we cleaned up everything down there, he ended up buying us a seventy-five-inch TV as a thank-you even though he had already let us use the space.

We had some furniture for the basement already, and we were going to get better stuff later on. But for the moment, everything was perfect and history was made—the basement was complete. I would tell Alyx about the basement all the time, but I talked about it like a little kid excited about something so she would laugh, but she thought it was a super cool thing. Alyx and I were still hanging out a lot but we would only hang out earlier in the day because of work. Alyx's coach from high school ran a concrete company and asked her if she wanted to work for him to build some money for college. It was a great opportunity, so she took it. Well, now, us hanging out was a lot harder, but we made it work.

CHAPTER 8

Heartbreak

Oh, also, since we are to the point where I can tell you, Alyx was going to one of the most expensive schools in Oregon. It was a really nice school, and she was going there to play volleyball and study physical therapy. I was going to work at the hospital because, uhh, yeah, I didn't get into any college that I applied for, and for some reason I had this thing against going to a community college. But really, it was because I didn't have the money. And if I had the money, I had no clue what I wanted to do. So I didn't think spending the money to go to a school to learn a bunch of shit that you don't know why you're learning it was worth it. Once I found out, everyone said it was OK, and of course I was saying, "Yeah, it's not that big of a deal," and moved on from the topic. But really, it broke me on the inside. I always told my grandparents growing up that I was going to do great things and go to college and get a great job so that they would be super proud of me, and I let them down. See, in my eyes, if I didn't go to college I was a lot lower than a lot of people. And trust me, once I found out, I treated myself like I was lower than everyone too.

I kept working at the hospital and Alyx kept doing concrete. I always wanted to go up and watch a sunset with someone who means a lot to me and just enjoy that moment. So, I told her that I wanted to make that a plan for us to do. She started to get really close with this guy she was working with, but I trusted her so it didn't bother me. It would throw me off when she told me she would go on walks with him after work, and she told me that she felt bad. But I told her that she shouldn't feel bad because she was just hanging out with a friend.

One night while I was working, Alyx got some food and went up to watch the sunset with some friends. It sucked 'cause I really wanted to do that with her, but, hey, can't always do everything together! The days went on, and Alyx and I hadn't seen each other in a while. We texted each other and talked every day but seeing each other in person hadn't happened in probably a month. One day while I was at work, I got a text from Alyx that read, "Hey, I'm really excited to see you and we should really sit down and talk." See, most of the time in my life when someone has told me, "Hey, let's sit down," it's usually a horrible thing. So, I asked her if it was a good talk or a bad talk, and she told me it was good. So, of course, I was still a little worried, but I told myself it would all be good!

After I was done with the workweek, we met up during the day at my house. She came inside for just a little bit to visit with my family, but after being at the house for a little while, she asked if we could go talk. There was a park by my house so we went on a walk to the park to talk. Once we got to the park, there was a bench where we sat to just catch up on how we've been since we hadn't seen each other in a while. The conversation was really good, and it was super nice to see her again. There was a break in the conversation, and that's when the tone and mood changed to be more serious. She started to talk about how she's going to college and how there wouldn't be any time for us and that she wanted to experience college. My argument was if you love somebody, you make time for them, and although it would be harder, we could give it a shot. I didn't comment on the college experience part, but in my head, I was telling myself she just wanted something new and she got bored. After I gave her my point of view, she understood what I was saying but she didn't agree.

I could feel my body temperature change as she said, "I think it's best if we move on from each other but always stay friends!" My lip started to curl up but not enough for her to see anything. I told her, of course, I would always be her friend and that everything was fine! We walked back to my house. I gave her a hug, and as I was walking away, she said, "Wait, give me one last kiss." So, I went over and did just that, she hopped in her car and left, and that was it.

I went to the front door, and as I grabbed the handle, I took a few deep breaths to calm my nerves before walking inside. I opened the door and my mom looked at me and says, "Hey, how was the talk with Alyx!?" I replied with a shaky voice, "Oh, it was good." She said, "Just good?" And before I could let out another word, I started bawling my eyes out. My parents and brother were asking me what was wrong, and that's when I muttered that we broke up. My whole family was shocked because they didn't think that was going to happen at all, but turns out they were wrong. They gave me the normal advice, ya know, there are plenty of fish in the sea so don't worry too much about it, you'll find the one. I got rid of my tears, and I was done sulking, at least in that moment.

So, when it comes to music, and this goes for anyone and everyone, you know how music makes you feel. Well, I listen to a lot of music. So, when it would come to night and no one was around, I would listen to sad music. Don't ask me why I did it 'cause I couldn't tell you. I've never cried over somebody like that. I mean, of course, people in my life have passed away and I've cried, but this was a different kind of pain. I was heartbroken and I didn't know what to do. Late at night, I would stay up and just cry until I fell asleep. It was a pain that I wouldn't want to wish upon anybody. I started to realize that it wasn't going to be something that went away in a day. Just slowly, over time, I would start to feel better. Once I started to feel better, there would be a random thing that would remind me of her or someone would talk about her and all of my emotions would be brought back again.

After a little while, I started to go on dates with other people, and they were good dates, but there was a really big problem. I thought I was ready, but I clearly wasn't because I was comparing every date I went on to Alyx and me when we were together. That's a really horrible thing to do especially if that person catches feelings for you, so I decided to stop for a while.

We still wanted to stay friends, and she was getting pretty close to college so we would still talk for a good amount of time. I started to realize we only ever talked if I texted her first, so I stopped texting. When that happened, we stopped talking altogether. We would check up on one another every once in a blue moon, but we weren't really friends anymore. Over time, I got over it, and I didn't have that pain I was feeling anymore, which was really nice but something still felt super off.

I realized that I might have been sad because I had a relationship that was now gone. But I think the thing that really hurt was the fact that there was no relationship at all anymore. I lost one of my closest friends, a person who I would open up to or talk to about literally anything with no worries. I didn't have them anymore, and that's what made it hurt the most. I told myself that it went both ways, and I did everything I could, and, I mean, there was no sense in watering a dead plant, so I forgot about it. After the breakup, I went on with life just like I did before. Now that the basement was finished, all of the guys and I were going over there a lot, which was really nice because it was like an escape. Whenever we went there, even if one of us did have something going on, you could talk about it and it wouldn't matter anymore.

I kept working at the hospital until I ended up having problems with the boss and a better opportunity came up. I went through this temp agency. Basically, a temp agency is a place that will interview you and if a place needs a worker, it'll send you there if you want to work. If you don't like it, then you can wait for the next best thing. When I got into it, I saw money and I lit up. To be honest, at this point I didn't really give a shit what I was doing as long as I was making bank. I saw a job to become a sheet metal roofer, and, I mean, I have no experience at all. But it was a newer company so it didn't mind taking me in and training me to see how I do. I met my foreman who was gonna be training me and his name was Mitch. As soon as I met him, I really liked the guy. Of course, he was older than me by a few years, but there was something about him that I just connected with. On our first job, we were working on a post office, and everything was going pretty damn well. I will say, though, that holding a big pallet of sheet metal by yourself on a windy day while someone takes you up on a roof in a boom lift isn't a very cool thing to me. That shit always sketched me out.

The days were going pretty well, and once we got on bigger jobs, I would make a lot more money, so I was looking forward to it. Once we finished that job, there was some guy who was building a shop, and his roof was a ten/twelve pitch, which is basically a fucking cliff, and we had to work on that fucking cliff. This was the day I found out that heights scared me. I guess it's not the heights but it's what happens if I fall from the heights that I wasn't a fan of. The main thing that Mitch kept telling me was I just had to trust my equipment. Well, I'm fucking sorry, Mitch, but I'm not gonna trust this rope with my life!! Every day on that job site was awful for me. The only thing that made it better was bullshitting with Mitch. I ended up talking to the main boss about it, but he told me to just keep trying and over time it'll get better. Mitch and I had to go on a trip for a job, which I thought was pretty cool. Maybe it would make me enjoy the job a little more because of the trip. I really enjoyed the trip and had a good time going into the town with Mitch and just messing around. The job wasn't too bad so I had no worries. Once we came back from the trip we had to go back to the shithole and work on that, and then I had enough. I ended up going on one more trip, and then I was done, which really sucked because I really enjoyed being around all of the guys I worked with. They were all great people. But at the end of the day, the job wasn't for me so I had to move on.

After that job, I was lost. I didn't have anything lined up and I sure as hell didn't know what I was going to do. So,

I began searching all over the place for jobs. I went from Craigslist to Indeed, and sometimes I would go into places and ask if they were hiring. I would look every day to just try and find a job that I actually enjoyed. I mean, sure, I didn't think I was gonna find my career through a Craigslist ad, but I just wanted something where when I woke up in the morning, I didn't hate it. The days then turned into weeks, and I couldn't afford to be out of work forever. My dad told me that AutoZone was hiring, so I applied and got an interview the next day. I never wanted to work there for multiple reasons, the big one being I don't know a fucking thing about cars! Unfortunately, the interview went great. I even told her that I didn't know anything about cars, but she didn't care. She said I was a super nice kid and that she would love to have me! See, in a fairy-tale world, when she offered me the job, I would have said: "Fuck no, I don't want to work here at all. It doesn't even crack my top twenty-five jobs for shitty things I'm gonna do until I call it quits!" But we don't live in a fairy-tale world and money doesn't grow on trees, so I took the job and was eager to learn!

My first couple days at AutoZone weren't bad because I just did testing and basically concluded that, hey, don't be a dick to customers! Once all the testing was finished, then I could move on and get trained in other areas of the store. The big problem was there weren't enough people working in the store, and if there were enough people, half of them didn't want to work. The store started to get really busy, and customers were lining up so I hopped on a register and started helping people. So, when it came to my training, I pretty much trained myself because nobody else had the time to do it. When it comes to people, I love them! I can't get enough of people. I think they're great, buutttt there are certain days where you just don't like people as much as you normally would, and this was one of those days. It was a pretty busy day, and I was working at the register when this older guy came up and asked for something. I helped him and there were no worries. He then came back and was ready to check out. While checking out, he asked for something and I said, "I'm sorry sir, what was that?" He then repeated it, and I had no fucking clue what he was talking about, so I asked him what it was. I will never ask somebody that again because once I asked, he then yelled at me and said, *"Are you a fucking idiot!?"* I wanted to hop over the counter and show the old fuck how much of an idiot I really was, but I stood there in shock! The manager then came out to the front, and instead of being a good manager, he said, "Well, you know that's why I get paid more because I know what's going on around here."

You know the part in the movie where the main character has a crazy thought and it plays out in the movie for a sec but then it pops back to reality? That's what happened to me. See, the manager was a bigger guy, so in my crazy movie moment, I wanted to say: "Yeah, you fat fuck, you get paid the big bucks so you don't eat the entire fucking store, you stupid piece of shit!" But then the crazy movie moment ended, and I was just shocked by what the manager just said. Anyway, on a day off, I was hanging out with some friends at the mall and these girls came up asking for our snaps. What I mean by snaps is Snapchat. If you don't know what Snapchat is, basically, it's an app you can text on but you send pics of yourselves to each other that can either last forever or three seconds. It's the dumbest app created to this existence and yet I still use it! I told the girls no, but my buddy ended up giving them mine anyway. Over a snap, she introduced me to her friend. Once I saw her, it was over. I was going to go after this girl no matter what. I thought she was stunning, so I got her snap and we started talking. The days at work were a lot better because half the time I was texting this girl trying to get to know her. Her name was Cassie, and she had me hooked. But the big problem was she lived in Smith and I lived in Thurston, which was about two hours away from Smith. Trying to find time to hang out was hard because she lived so far away. But we found time and ended up meeting each other after talking over the phone for a while. We went to a drive-in movie theater for our first date, which was cool because I got to finally meet her in person and I always wanted to go to a drive-in movie. I thought it was gonna be super awkward at first, but we clicked in person and the conversation never died which was great! After the date, I had a long, late drive home, and I don't regret a single second of it.

We started hanging out more and more and then she told me about a prom she had coming up. I thought it would be super fun because I never got a prom, and I could invite all the guys. I talked to all of them about it, and the boys and I were gonna take a road trip. All of us got dressed up really nice, and Dalton was going with Cassie's friend, and Jake was kinda going with another one of their friends, so it worked out better 'cause now it wasn't just me with a date to the prom. Once we got to Cassie's house, we all took pictures and visited, and then it was time for their dance. We couldn't go to their prom because COVID was still a thing, but we were gonna have a party after the dance so it was still pretty good. While the girls were at the dance, we all checked into our hotel rooms. The rooms were a lot nicer than we thought they were going to be. Each room had two queen beds, so we got two rooms and we were all going to share. After all of the driving and talking, by the time we checked into our rooms, we were all worn out. But we didn't have any time to nap because we had to go pick the girls up from the dance. We picked the girls up and then we went to eat. The girls wanted to go to Shari's, so that's where we went. I still don't really know why we went there because nobody really ordered anything. The guys and I ordered a shitty Oreo pie shake; the girls got water, and one girl got a plate full of hashbrowns. Once Shari's was over, we went to one of their family friend's property where there was a pretty big barn. We ended up throwing a little party at the barn and it was a good time! After the party, we told the girls they could come hang out at the hotel for a little if they wanted to. All of us were having a good time at the hotel rooms, and then Cassie and I went to one of the rooms and started to do what young teenagers do. We wanted to be all over each other. But while this was happening, she stopped and looked at me and said, "Hunter I love you." Before I go on, let me give you a word of advice: don't ever say those eight letters unless you truly mean it because you'll know if you mean it or not. In this situation, I panicked and said, "I love you too, Cassie!" I did not love her, I liked her a lot, but I didn't want to tell her I didn't love her and hurt her feelings. So, instead of telling her the truth, I told her what she wanted to hear. The next morning, we all went and ate breakfast but something just felt off, and I think it was the fact that I told somebody I loved them when I didn't mean it. By the time we all got home, we were all exhausted and the next day was work for all of us so we ended up calling it a day.

When we got back, I kept working at AutoZone until I realized the hours were shit, I wasn't making any money, and the money I did make was all going to bills. So, I started looking for jobs again. I saw Walmart was hiring for seventeen dollars an hour, and when I heard that my ears perched up like a dog. I thought, "Shit, an easy walk-in-the-park job for some good cash, no problem!" I went into Walmart and applied for an online shopper position. As an online shopper, my goal was to shop for the groceries people ordered in a timely manner and put everything where it was supposed to be. They said it was a pretty fast-paced job so I was looking forward to it. Once I started the job, of course, I was lost, but after a couple weeks of training I pretty much got the job down. During lunch in the breakroom, I hated it because while you're in there it's like everybody is a zombie. Being in the breakroom could put a person in a bad mood, so I would go to my truck during my breaks and talk to Cassie on the phone.

When I applied for Walmart, I told them I would need time off because the guys and I were all planning on taking a trip to Sunriver. Everybody in the group has been there but me, and we all wanted to go on a trip so we chose to go there. To sum up, Sunriver is a really nice place. It's got a little village with a bunch of little shops and people can rent houses and stay there to kinda just get away from their problems. We planned the trip a while ago, and it was finally time to go—a full week on our own, just all the guys hanging out. The trip was pretty damn great. The house that we rented came with bikes so we would ride the bikes all over Sunriver, go play basketball, chill in the hot tub, and a shit ton of other things. My favorite time throughout the whole trip was close to the last day. It was getting closer to night and we started playing music and cooking up some burgers. After we were done eating, we all went on the golf course at Sunriver and started playing football. I think the reason why I enjoyed it so much was because it made me feel like a little kid camping with the family again, which was a feeling I forgot about.

There's a waterpark at Sunriver, nothing crazy big, but it's a decent-sized waterpark. On our last day, we all went to the waterpark until about noon. Then we rushed back to the house to clean up and take care of the place. Then it was time to go home. Dalton rode with me on the way up and he rode with me on the way back. The drive back was great as we were jamming out to old rock music and talking about the entire trip as if it happened years ago. Then, like that, the trip was over and we were home.

Once I got back to work, a lot of people thought I didn't work there anymore because they didn't know about the vacation. I went on with work, but every day was a challenge because my mental health was slowly fading away.

CHAPTER 9

Rock Bottom

There's nothing wrong with working at Walmart. I mean, really, it's a pretty good job. It pays well, and for a young kid, that's all you need. In my head, that's what I'm trying to tell myself, but that is not at all what's going on. If I told somebody that I don't compare myself to other people, well, then, fucking shoot me on sight 'cause I'm the biggest liar in the world. I used to not compare myself to other people, but now I do it all the time, and that's the biggest reason why my brain is saying Walmart is bad. If anyone asks what I've been up to, I look at them and say, "Oh, I'm working at Walmart," while there are kids my age who are in college pursuing great careers or making music, acting—superstars, ya know, the whole fucking nine. There're all these young kids doing these great things or going after something. And then there's me who is just working at Walmart with not a clue of what I'm gonna do for the rest of my life. I kept telling myself that every day I went to work, not because I wanted to get myself down on purpose, but because mentally I was starting to lose the fight, and I couldn't stay as positive as I once could.

Now, I know at this point you're probably thinking: "What the fuck is wrong with this kid? He's young, he shouldn't have any worries!" Well, just hold on one sec because I need to introduce you to a friend of mine named Rock Bottom, the name of this chapter. Huh, isn't that convenient? When I got dumped by Alyx, I didn't think it could get much worse than that. What a fucking idiot I was for thinking that a girl was going to be the worst of my problems. I think that the biggest battle anyone can have will always be with themselves. You know how I was saying I was starting to lose that mental battle with myself? Well, uhh, yeah, I lost. I didn't want to go to work because I hated it so much, and I hated the fact that I was doing nothing with my life. So, one night I decided to change that. Let me introduce you to another pal of mine called hydrocodone, also known as Norco. If you look up the definition for Norco, it'll tell you it's a painkiller. But it also says if taken in high doses, it could cause death. My mom has a really bad back. When she was younger, she got in a car accident and had surgery on it and she's had multiple surgeries on her back since then. So, my mom takes Norco to help with the pain, but my mom's Norco is a little stronger than that regular shit because that regular shit doesn't quite do the job.

One night it was late, probably around 2:00 in the morning, and I couldn't sleep. I tried everything I possibly could to sleep but my mind just kept going and I couldn't get any rest. So, I got out of bed and just went into the living room. Well, I've taken Norco before for pain, and I know it can make you sleepy, so as a last resort, I took a pill. Any pill in the world if you want it, well, it's right there on top of our microwave. Whether it be ibuprofen or Norco, we got it right on top of our microwave, so I went to the microwave and took one pill. After I took the pill, I went back to bed, but I still couldn't sleep. So, I went back and took another pill. By the end of the night, I probably took about five Norcos. I slept like a rock. I woke up the next morning and went to work like everything was all good. On break, I called Cassie. We laughed, had a good talk, and then I went home to chill with the family. But this mental battle with myself was getting worse and worse by the second. Once again, late at night, I can't sleep, so I go and pop a Norco. But this time I just dumped them in my hand and popped them like they were candy. As I go back to bed and lay there, my whole body's numb and I feel like I'm just floating there. My ears feel stuffy and I can feel all the blood rushing through my head. I still can't sleep, so I stumble out of the bed walking as if I just got off of the Gravitron to the microwave to take just a little more. After I took the pills, I counted a total of thirteen. I woke up the next morning vomiting my guts up in a toilet, sicker than a dog. When my parents saw, they said, "Oh dang, you must have got food poisoning." And with a simple look at them, I nod in agreement like the snake I am. Oh, and guess what? I'm sick, which means no work, which means I hate life a little less today.

I know you might not like me very much at the moment, and I don't blame you. I mean, I'm being selfish and an awful human being. Like really, though! I'm not lying, I'm doing bad things to myself, but at this point, I don't give a shit! While I'm in an argument between me and my mind, I ask myself, "Do you want to die?" The sane part, which is the real me, is saying: "Fuck no, I don't want to die. I have so much more to do and see in this world, and it's not my time yet." But the depression in my brain is saying: "Well, I don't want to kill myself, but if I died, maybe it would be like a fresh start. And if I died, I wouldn't have all of these problems that I have right now." I was to the point where life didn't matter to me, and if life doesn't matter, then nothing matters. If I wasn't popping pills to sleep, then I was crying myself to sleep. It was one or the other. There would be moments where I would be with my family or friends where it wasn't total darkness and the sunshine would come out. But once that moment was over, it was back to darkness. The big problem was since I was depressed, I didn't want to do anything. So, if there were moments to get out and be happy, I didn't really care too much to go do those things.

When it came to other people's lives and feelings, I was still there for them. I would never want the people I love and care about to be hurt or feel bad in any type of way. But when it came to my life, I didn't care. I've beaten severe depression before, but even when you "beat" depression, it still lingers. It never truly goes away; it's just waiting for you to slip up and have multiple bad days until you finally give in to it. Well, this was a depression I was feeding into and I was giving it everything I had from every bone to every feeling. It wasn't mine anymore, and the hardest part about it is that it's all on me. If someone says, "Yeah I've been depressed," and they tell you to just think in a positive mindset and it'll go away—fuck them because clearly they've never been depressed.

All right, all the uneducated bitches out there who are like, "OMG, I don't understand why people are depressed, just be happy," well, I'm gonna teach you some shit in the best way I can explain it. If you smoke cigarettes and one day I say, "Hey, you need to stop smoking; that's bad for you," well, you're probably gonna tell me to fuck off. That's because you're addicted, so you can't just stop on a dime like that. It takes time and help. Well, look at depression as a drug. Your brain has had so many negative thoughts that it's hooked on all the negatives, there are no positives. If there is a positive, well, it's not good enough. That's why people can't just be happy. It takes time and help whether people like to admit that or not, they need help. It's a battle you can't beat alone.

There was one night where I had the pills in my hand and I went to get the alcohol. But I didn't do it even though I felt like giving up and drinking a bunch of alcohol with a bunch of pills. Clearly, my will to live beat my will to die. After a couple of weeks longer at Walmart, I was done. I left and afterward I was just as lost as I was before, but I felt a little bit of something lift off of my shoulders. I now didn't have a job, but I took a little bit of time off to try to gather myself. I hung out with Cassie and played video games with the guys. I would edit videos and post them on YouTube whether people liked them or not. It brought me joy, and if it made other people laugh, it made me even happier. I started looking for jobs again and found this car detailing job. I went into the shop and I just started working under the table for cash, which was fine. But I wanted to be hired on, and since that wasn't happening, I continued looking for jobs while working at the detail shop.

While looking on Craigslist, I came across an ad that stated "Paint Old School Muscle Cars." I saw that ad and it sounded sick, so I messaged the person who posted the ad. Later on in the day, Kade, Jake, Brody, and I went to Buffalo Wild Wings for dinner. While we were sitting there eating dinner, I saw these three girls walk in. The first girl had blond hair, brown pants, a black top, with big black boots. To be honest, the other two are kind of a blur when it comes to what they were wearing. But I noticed these girls as soon as they walked in because you don't see girls like this every day. And before you call me a piece of shit, yes, I have a girlfriend. I'm not into them, I'm just saying they're pretty girls. After our dinner, we were heading out to our cars to head to the basement when we heard "Don't Stop Believing" by Journey and girls singing the song coming from a car that was parked next to Brody's truck. I don't know why but once we heard the music, we decided to chill in the parking lot in the back of Brody's truck and sing along to their music with them.

After a few songs, the girls rolled their car window down, and inside sat the three girls I saw walk into Buffalo Wild Wings. With the music going, all of us kinda looked at each other while nodding our heads to the music, and then we kinda talked to one another as if we were at a party and you just met somebody for the first time. They asked if we were from around the area, and we told them that we grew up here. They then asked if we were going to the university. I replied, "Oh no, we're too stupid for that." The blond one said: "Oh no, you're not. Don't say that." She chuckled as she said it. After shouting from one another's cars a little longer, they finally got out. The blond girl came to the side of the bed of Brody's truck with her hand out and said, "Hi, my name's Haily." I then told her my name and then hopped out of the bed of the truck. Once we were all on ground level, we met the other two. They both had brown hair and one of them was like six-four. Her name was Sarah and the other one was Ella. They told us that they were freshmen at the university and they were playing volleyball. Haily was from Oregon but the other two weren't. Sarah was from San Diego and Ella was from San Francisco. I didn't know many people from different places so it was kinda cool meeting some people from new places. The conversations just kept going on, whether it was as a whole group or separate conversations. There were a few moments where it got quiet, but they would soon go away because there was music playing.

While talking to them, you could read their personalities. All of them were outgoing, but Sarah was very outgoing and could talk up a storm with you about anything. She wasn't a person who pretended to be into what you were saying. She genuinely cared. Haily had a super bubbly personality, and she laughed a lot, which was cool because I did that. So, if there was ever a quiet moment that night, either my or her laughter would help lighten things up. Ella, I couldn't read too much because she was pretty quiet compared to the other girls. She stayed really close to them, and because of that, I think she's a person where the more she knows you, the more talkative and brighter she gets! After Buffalo Wild Wings, we were supposed to go over to the basement to meet Dalton. But by now, we've been in the parking lot for about two hours, so Jake called Dalton and told him what was going on. And of course, Dalton didn't believe it, so he drove down to Buffalo Wild Wings to check it out for himself. Once he got there, everybody introduced themselves, and then for about another two hours we ended up dancing in the parking lot, listening to music, talking, laughing, and everyone was having a good time.

Before they left, we got each other's Instagrams, and Sarah said she was gonna make a group chat with everyone in it and we would all hang out soon. Once we got to the basement, we were talking about the night and how fucking crazy it was that we just hung out in a parking lot for four hours dancing to music with three strangers that we just met. Then we were talking about the odds of Sarah making a group chat and all of us actually hanging out again. I guess the odds were pretty good because at about that time, everybody got a notification on their phones with the name of "The Douchebags" with a text from Sarah that said, "What up fellow Douches!" Once in the group chat, all of us looked at each other with disbelief because we all thought it was just gonna be a quick thing. Little did we know we were about to become good friends with them!

While sitting in awe, we needed to find a time to meet up with them because we figured if we didn't, then things would fall through and that would be it! So, in the group chat we asked if they wanted to meet at the park and play beach volleyball. We figured they wouldn't say no because it was volleyball! Then the next day, we all met at the park and played for a little bit, but it was more than just playing volleyball. It became visiting with one another and learning more about each other. I mean, within the day, I already knew more about them than kids I went to school with! All of us were pretty stoked about the day, and we all just hoped the friendship would keep growing!

I know I titled this chapter "Rock Bottom," which is true. But, I mean, it can't all be bad. That's why I started talking about the girls that we met and stuff. Anyway, on to the next chapter!

CHAPTER 10

A Summer to Remember

After the quick beach volleyball game, we all ended up hitting it off. We started hanging out more and things were great! After a little while, we went over to their apartment to hang out where they had another friend that we hadn't met yet. Her name was Hope. When we first met her, we all kinda had a bad first impression because she wasn't in the best mood. But the only reason for that was because the night before she drank for the first time and had a decent amount and she was paying for it!

So, you know how in the last chapter I said I messaged some guy about painting old-school muscle cars? Well, after I applied for the job, I got a text from Brody's dad, which was strange because Will (Brody's dad) never texts me. In the text, he said, "Hey, did you just apply for a painter job on Craigslist?" I replied, "Yeah why what's up?" So, Will is a painter on a TV show called *Graveyard Carz*. It's like the biggest Mopar TV show in the country and I just applied to be his helper. We talk about it for a little while, but tensions become high because ever since Brody was a kid, he always wanted to work with his dad. But Will said he would never do it. Now that Brody knows that I might have the job, he's pissed! He always wanted this job, and now he thinks he's getting cheated out of it. And here I am, just looking for a job not expecting to be working for Will! After a couple of days of thinking and talking, Will comes up with an idea because he really wanted to hire me but he didn't wanna leave Brody in the dust since he has wanted the job forever. So Will told me I'll be working in the engine room with Doug, and Brody will work with Will painting. I didn't really care where I was going to work as long as I got the job, although I did really want to paint the cars, it wasn't that big of a deal to me like it was to Brody. The only thing I was a little nervous about was the fact that I was working on cars and didn't really know much about them.

I was then relieved because they told me I didn't need to know much about cars because they would teach me a lot. They just told me to pay attention and work hard. That was easy enough, so I was super stoked about the job! Although life was going well, Cassie and I broke up. To be honest, I just wasn't into it. I feel like I lost feelings, which is a bad thing to say but it's the truth. Although it was hard to do, I felt like it was for the best!

The Lane County Fair was coming up, and all the guys wanted to go to it because we hadn't been for a while. While we were there, we ran into Haily and Ella, so we ended up spending the rest of the night at the fair with them. I'm not much of a ride person, but if I get peer-pressured enough, then I'll do it. But it's pretty tough! Everyone wanted to go on the Zipper, which is this ride where there are two people in a cage with six cages. It then goes clockwise while your cage is also spinning. Oh yeah, and it goes like fifty feet in the air! I don't know why I went on the ride, but I ended up doing it. Jake and Levi were in a cage, Dalton and Kade, and then Haily and me. When I'm terrified, most of the time, I don't scream. But in this case, I was terrified and felt really nauseous so I didn't say a thing. I just held on for dear life with my eyes closed. As the ride is going on, Haily is screaming at the top of her lungs, and I manage to whimper, "Haily, it's fine!" Which just made me feel even more sick to my stomach.

Finally, the ride was over, and once I was out, I felt like I couldn't walk, and I'm trying to figure out how to walk again. Dalton and Kade talked about how they spun the cage so fast their phones fell out of their pockets and started bouncing off of their faces. Even though it was terrifying, it was the first time I'd ever been on a ride like that so I was going to remember that for a long time.

As the days went on, I found myself always doing something, whether that be hanging with the girls, work, or working on YouTube. No matter what it was, my mind was always occupied. So I was never depressed or made myself sad 'cause there was no way for my mind to bring me down.

We went to the girls' apartment for a little party they were having. I saw Hope again and started to give her a hard time. She said, "I bet you don't even remember my name," and she followed it with a witty laugh. I responded: "Are you kidding? You're Hope. How could I forget your name!?" That night, I don't know what it was, but I just liked her. I mean, of course, she was attractive, but it wasn't that I wanted to date her. Just her vibe was really cool!

After the night of the party, Hope and I started texting a lot more and just kinda getting to know each other. Only problem with this was that every night we were out with each other till three to four in the morning just talking about music, our lives, our opinions, or just anything to keep the conversation going until we both realized it was getting too late so we had to go home because she had school and I had work. We started talking and hanging out more and more. I realized I was super into her and wanted to be more than friends. I never really told her how I felt, but I think she knew.

Coming up was the State Fair, and all of us wanted to go mostly because a lot of us had never been before. Everybody was going except Brody because I think he had plans. The drive up to the fair was great with lots of laughs and loud, random music. I mean, you couldn't ask for anything better! Once we got to the fair, it was packed! There were so many people in line to pay for the overpriced State Fair just like us! After waiting in line for about half an hour we were finally in.

For some reason, Dalton, Hope, and I kinda went and did our own thing. After that, we started to meet up with the group. As we were walking through the fair, a group of three or four guys ran up to Hope and Haily and were basically begging them to slap one of them for a YouTube video. He was pretty persistent about it. They ended up saying no, but, I mean, if he would have asked me, I would have done it! I mean, whatever you gotta do to get the bag!

As the fair went on, we were playing a ton of games. Speaking of which, Ella was a *god* at the basketball game. She won like two huge stuffed animals, and she wasn't allowed to do it anymore. That's how good she was!

Dalton, Hope, Sarah, and I were waiting in line for this ride called the Kamikaze. I swear we waited all day to go on this ride, and then when we got pretty close to the front, we didn't do it! I mean, it was probably for the best 'cause I was only gonna do it 'cause Hope wanted to do it. But, oh God, this ride looked terrifying!

At the end of the night, we ended up getting on a few rides, nothing too crazy, but they were a lot of fun. On the rides, I ended up sitting next to Ella instead of Hope, which is not what I wanted. But overall, it was a great night with a lot of memories!

After the State Fair, Hope and I talked because she thought that I had a thing for Ella and not her, which, I mean, was kind of great to hear because that meant she liked me! For the rest of the time we talked, it was just like before except we both knew how each other felt, so the night was great! We went to Ella's birthday party the next month and I ended up kissing Hope, which, of course, was great. But I didn't like it because I had this feeling in the back of my mind that we just were going to be a thing, which is fine 'cause that's just how my brain works. But since I kissed her, my feelings grew even more than they had before. After that kiss, it was never really the same, and we started talking to each other less one night. She invited me over to just talk about things, and she said she really likes me, she just wasn't ready.

Come to find out, I just wasn't tall enough. At least, that's what Ella and Sarah told me. Oh yeah, just so everybody knows, I'm a little over six-one. I've never really been self-conscious about my height because, I mean, I can't control that, and overall, I'm pretty tall! But holy shit, I'm *too short*!? Are you fucking kidding me? What am I supposed to do? Plus, she was only a little bit taller than me. But it's cool. Whatever! Just don't look over in the corner of the room because that's where I'll be crying. Fast-forward a long way and now she's dating like a six-four guy. If he was ugly, I could say something, but he's far from it, sooo yeah, moral of the story, I'm a short king!

Anyway, after all of that went down, I started hanging out with Ella and Sarah a lot more than anybody else. The main thing that we did was Kade, Jake, Sarah, Ella, and I would all go on long drives. Every once in a while, Dalton or Brody would come, but most of the time it was just that group. We would go on drives to Portland at seven and wouldn't come back till three thirty, five thirty in the morning. We were doing this like every night!

Then I started to have a thing for Ella, and we would cuddle all the time or I would stay the night at her dorm or yada, yada, yada, and nothing ever happened. I was getting played like a guitar! She was never into me, so I don't know why we were ever trying in the first place. It's clear to say I was making my rounds through the friend group. Not on purpose, things were just happening and feelings were growing!

Although all of this was happening, we were all still really good friends. We would go to their volleyball games and cheer them on, and sometimes afterward everybody would hang out with one another. The only two people who didn't like each other were Brody and Sarah. When all of us first met, Brody had a big crush on Sarah, and he really wanted to date her. But she said she had too much going on during the volleyball season. So, he said that it was cool and after the season he would try again, which, I mean, in my book sounds like a good idea!

During the season, Brody and Sarah started hanging out a lot and not in a group-setting type of way but just them-alone-doing-shit type of way. I thought it was cool because I thought that maybe Sarah was starting to like Brody, but she never did! Then the more and more they hung out, Brody's feelings kept growing but Sarah kept hanging out with him even though she knew that. Personally, I think Brody found his first love, and because of that, it made him crazy about her, as it should! Brody ended up trying one more time, but it was a little pushy and Sarah blew up on him. After that, Sarah didn't like Brody and Brody didn't like Sarah.

I was always kind of pissed at how things ended because neither of them could just be straight-up honest with how they felt, and then it turned into this! See, kids, this is a great example of just speaking what's on your mind but do it in a nice way, not a dickhead way! We were still hanging out together but you could tell that the group was slowly drifting apart. Then it was kinda weird because one day all of it kinda just stopped. I would text some of them but it was a super quick conversation and it never really went more than a couple texts and then the conversation was over! They were people who I thought were going to be in my life forever, and then out of nowhere, *poof*, gone. On birthdays and stuff, we would talk and just give a quick "Happy Birthday!" But if I ever wanted to talk to anyone, I had to text first, which kinda sucked 'cause after a while it was annoying, so I stopped.

I've always been a person who wants to try new things and meet new people, but I guess I've never had the opportunity to do that. I also never put myself out there enough to have that opportunity. Now don't get me wrong, I'm a big extrovert. But I guess I was just content with my life and didn't need anything else. Which in my book is a really bad thing because I'm the type of person who always wants more or who is never content. But it's safe to say that I was just stuck! Being with the girls that summer changed my life in so many ways. I know to a lot of you it might not seem like that much or that big of a deal. But in my life, I've never been out like that before and met so many new faces and talked to so many new people and just got thrown out of my comfort zone more than ever! They helped me out of that rut. If I was still super close with all of them, I still might be doing the same thing as I was doing instead of going out and trying to do something else! Although the way things ended was pretty shitty, I will forever remember the girls and I'll still try and reach out and hang with them even if I have to start the conversation. Because at the end of the day, they honestly changed my life. That's what certain people do. So many people are going to come into your life and some are meant to stay. In this case, they came into my life and changed it for the better but they weren't meant to stay, which is fine. You just have to learn to be content with that.

But now, summer was finally coming to an end. It was a weird feeling because for me, I never really had a summer because I still kept working and everything else. Now it was just time for everyone to start going back to school and for the weather to get worse! Even though people were going back to school and most people would have less time for things, I was still in a really good mood. I mean, the last couple months had been great, and I felt like I couldn't come down from that feeling! It was probably the happiest I've been in a long time!

CHAPTER 11

Old Habits and New Beginnings

Life kept going on about the same as it always had, now it was just a little less exciting because we weren't hanging out with the girls anymore. Although it was the same, I still wanted more in life. Everything went back to the way it was before, just rinse and repeat the same thing every day, nothing new to it, and me not doing anything about it. The only thing that was different about it this time was that I was in a good mood, which scared me because I was content. Now, I know it's not completely true, but I always say I'm scared of getting comfortable because once you get comfortable, you're going to do the same thing for the rest of your life. The reason I say it's not completely true is because one day down the road you're going to want to settle down. At that point in your life, you should be comfortable, and you most likely will be doing the same thing for the rest of your life or until you retire. But at the end of the day, that's really not that bad of a thing! I mean, shit, that's the American dream right!? But you see, what I'm scared of is being content or comfortable right now at a really young age and then not impacting the world in any sort of way and doing the same thing until I'm dead and never getting to live the life that I want! Now, I know it's a little supererogatory but that's just how my brain works!

Dalton was coming to a close on his sophomore year of college, and after the first two years at a community college, he was going to go to a university. He just wasn't quite sure which one he wanted to go to. He didn't know if he wanted to stay local or switch it up completely and go out of state. Growing up, my parents always told me that if Dalton left, I would leave because Dalton's my best friend, and they thought that if he was to leave, I'd find a way to go with. He was going to stay in state, but it was more expensive than for him to go out of state to Idaho. He's always talked about Idaho, and he and his family always liked it. But he'd never been to Moscow, Idaho, where the University of Idaho is located. (It was pronounced Moscoe but spelled like Moscow.) He wasn't quite set on going, but he wanted to visit first. So, he and his family took a trip up there for a little over a weekend to see how he liked it.

When he got back, while he was talking about it, you could tell he really enjoyed it. Dalton is not much of a big-city type of person, and Moscow was far from it, so he really liked that part. He said it kinda had a homey vibe and that all of the people there were really nice. To me, it sounded like he was sold.

As the days went on, we stopped talking about it until one day it was brought up. He said he really wanted to go, but he didn't wanna go alone because it would be a completely new place and he would have to take on all of that alone. He then started to talk to Kade, Brody, and me about going with him. We were gonna talk to Jake but we knew he wouldn't go because of his work at his dad's business. Overall, I figured Brody wouldn't go because I talked to him about it for a little bit and he said he didn't want to leave his little sister, Leila, and he wasn't financially stable enough to go even though none of us were because we were all twenty years old.

So that left Kade and me. Even though I wanted to try something new and get out of my comfort zone, this was a really big step for me. I could only imagine how Kade felt because maybe I'm wrong, but in my eyes, Kade was pretty content with what he was doing in life, and he just got a girlfriend, Kiara, who we all knew. But, I mean, for him, life was good! If we were to move to Idaho with Dalton, we needed to see the place first, so we ended up taking a road trip. It was our first-ever road trip like that alone, which was pretty cool! By this point, my parents were flipping out because I feel like every kid's parents want them to move out and go forward in life but once that gets close to happening or just an idea of it, then the parents become sad and almost mad even though they aren't there, just scared of losing their baby.

On our road trip, there were two towns we were going to see—Lewiston, Idaho, and Moscow. Dalton was more of a fan of Moscow, but he said he was looking at a school in Lewiston too, so we were gonna check them both out. The road trip was pretty fun just because we were all together and it was our first one but it was very long. Finally, after a long drive, we made it to Lewiston. That's where we were staying for the night, and then the next day, we were going to explore. Once we got to our hotel, the night consisted of Dalton and Kade wrestling a lot, like a shit ton, and all of us going down to the pool to mess around, and then going upstairs and passing out because of how tired we all were.

The next morning when we woke up, that's when Kade and I were gonna see if we liked the place. As we wandered through Lewiston, I came up with a decision within the first fifteen minutes of seeing things as to if I was going to move there. The answer was no! I didn't like Lewiston. No offense to anyone who lives in Lewiston, but to me, it was boring. There was nothing there that was grabbing my attention to make me stay, and it was just like my hometown but not as nice. Now, if I was around there, I would probably visit, but I wouldn't live there for life or a short period of time. Now, Moscow was only forty minutes away from Lewiston so we spent the next day in Lewiston then we were headed for Moscow. Although I didn't like Lewiston, it had some good-ass restaurants that we ate at, and it was the first time I'd ever done anything like that, so overall it was still fun being in Lewiston. Just like I said, not my thing.

Next up was Moscow, and I'm not gonna lie to you, as soon as we got there, I really liked it. It was this sort of old-school, new-school downtown-type place, and I just really like the way everything looked and how it was all set up. When we first got there, all of us were super hungry. The first place we saw looked like a giant Airstream. It was this old-school diner. As you walk in, the floors are checkered, they have the classic booths to sit at that you would see in a Coca-Cola painting, and to top it off, they had the classic music playing! A very bright woman with blond hair was our waitress. As soon as we told her we'd never eaten there before, her face lit up, and she gave us a rundown of everything and then started visiting with us about where we were from and the whole nine.

After eating lunch, we drove around for a little bit because we couldn't check into our motel for a little while.

While driving around Moscow, it reminded me a little of downtown Springfield, which is about fifteen minutes away from my house. The one thing I noticed was that it's clean. Now, Springfield isn't dirty and downtown Springfield isn't that bad. But when it comes to Eugene, it is dirty. I love Eugene, so many people hate it, but you can't avoid the fact that it's really dirty, and there are a lot of homeless people, which overall is really sad. Some places are like that and some aren't, and Moscow is far from it!

The place we were staying at was called the Monarch Motel and that place was sick! It had this cool, modern, rustic look, and for the price, it was a solid room! Now here's the thing with me. Like I was saying earlier: music is everything, so when I hear a song and it fits what I'm feeling, I'm gonna melt. It's now night and as we're driving back to downtown Moscow, a song comes on I've never heard before. Down the strip, the trees have lights tangled through them with snow on the ground and people walking around with hot cups of coffee or hot chocolate. I felt very calm and relaxed in the moment, something I haven't felt in a long time, but even this was better. I almost had the feeling I could fly because of how at ease I felt. Then, the song ended and it was whatever! That's how much power a song held over me. I think the reason for that was sadness and fear of the fact that I was most likely going to be moving here.

The next day when we all woke up, we were going to check out a place called the Grove. Most of the younger kids lived there. There were still older people, but it was cheap for younger people. Most of the time, it was pretty full and hard to get in because people would re-sign the lease pretty fast. We got a tour, and they had a beach volleyball court, a gym, a clubhouse with a pool table, ping-pong table, and shuffleboard, and then to top it off, they had a pool! The place was pretty damn cool, especially for the price! It was still going to cost us but not like it would back home.

After spending the next couple days there, it was finally time to go back home. On the drive back, we kept talking about everything we liked and all of the possibilities on what we're going to do and how everyone was feeling about all of it. I liked it a lot and I knew Dalton was going to go so I was pretty much in. But something inside of me wasn't ready yet. I mean, of course, I looked confident from the outside and talked a big game, but on the inside, I was like a lost dog. I didn't know what I was going to do, why I would go, and why I wouldn't go. My mind started jumping all over the place!

After a long drive back, we all finally got home. Once my mom saw me, there was a sigh of relief to see I was OK and mostly just back home. My dad got right into it. "So, what did you think?" God's honest truth, I didn't really know. I mean, I sort of knew, but not fully. I told him and my mom I really liked the place but there's a lot to think about. With those words, my mom went into a panic. "Well, what do you mean there's a lot to think about!?" she said. I then responded: "Mom, it's fine. There's a lot I have to think about because I might go, I might not." The big problem overall was I didn't have much time to think. We had about two and a half to three months to sign the lease, and even then, we were not guaranteed to get a place because it might be full sooner than that. So I had to come up with a decision to move, and not just move out of my parents' house—with whom I've lived with since I was born—to a different house down the road, but I was going to move out of state, and I had two months to figure it out! This was far from an easy decision because all of the people I loved and knew live in Oregon. And I actually really enjoyed my job now. I wouldn't do it for the rest of my life but it was the first time in a while I didn't hate waking up in the morning, and I would have to leave all of that and start over!

The whole thing was really stress-inducing. I felt like if I left, people would be disappointed or it would make them upset in some way. After a couple weeks or close to a month, I told my parents I was gonna do it. Their main questions were what's the difference between there and here, and why do I wanna do it? I told them overall, there wasn't much of a difference, but I asked them if they were my age and had the opportunity to move into a place with some of their best friends, would they do it? Of course, they responded with yes. I then told them I might as well do it while I'm young because I won't do anything like this when I'm older! They completely agreed even though it was terrifying for all of us, and it was gonna be hard. Sooner or later, everyone has to move out, and the earlier you leave, the easier it's gonna be later on!

My nana ended up passing away. She was my mom's mom, which was very sad. I've lost a lot of people at a young age, so I would like to tell you it's easier, but it's not. It never is. I can't even imagine losing my parents, so I can only imagine what my mom felt that night that she passed away, which is what almost made me cry, but I somehow didn't. My nana was an amazing woman and an even better person, so if she was here for what I'm about to tell you, she would be really disappointed in me. So, as I made the decision to move and my nana just passed away, my mind was always going, and now I was thinking about everything even more than I was before, and it kept me up real late at night. Now this chapter is called "Old Habits and New Beginnings" for I think pretty obvious reasons! I was up late one night and I remembered hydrocodone (Norco) would help me sleep. I also liked the way it made me feel, but in this case, it was going to help me sleep. It helped me sleep a little bit, but since I've taken it so much before I needed something stronger or just more, so I took a little more and went to bed. Well, you see, although I was happy about getting to experience life with my buddies and moving out for the first time ever, deep inside I hated myself, and I still felt like I wasn't going to do anything to impact the world. After I took those pills, it was like I was back to square one all over again, and my mental health took a drop. But I was really good at hiding it, so the only person who knew my mental health took a drop was me.

    I started back up with doing pills, but this time Norco wasn't strong enough, and my mom's pills were running low so I had to stop taking them or it would look obvious. So, before my nana passed away, she was getting sick and had a lot of pain so there were a lot of pills she was taking. Well, after she passed away, we had her meds in our medicine cabinet in a Ziplock bag. I didn't know what she was taking, but I knew she had some kind of painkillers that were strong, so at night I would go up and look. The first one I found was tramadol, which is a really strong painkiller mostly used for severe pain or pain right after surgery. I looked up the side effects of taking it, and holy hell, there were a lot! It was like at the end of one of those medicine commercials where the guys say all of the symptoms really fast. Now, the other downside to tramadol is you can get addicted really easily. So, because I've never taken any before, I took two of them and went to bed. When I woke up, I was still feeling it, and it gave me that feeling of I didn't care. So, I liked it because all I would think about before would be negative thoughts and getting down on myself. But with this, I didn't think of anything. I started to take a couple before work, and it made the day go by fast. But it got to the point I hated going through the day without it. Even though I was doing all of this, I would still work out with the guys and still go and edit YouTube videos. Doing that stuff made me really happy, so I should've just focused on that. But I was letting my brain win, and I was done fighting 'cause I didn't really care anymore.

Now here's where it gets worse, not bad because it's already bad, but a lot worse! I stopped taking the tramadol because now that bottle was getting a little low. So I went back into the Ziplock bag and found a different thing that goes by the name of Xanax. Xanax is used to treat anxiety, panic attacks, and insomnia. I took one at night and slept like a rock. But for some stupid reason, I took it before work. A safe amount of Xanax in a day is about .25 milligrams spread out three times throughout the day. But some are stronger, like in this case. I'm not quite sure what it was, but my nana's were significantly stronger.

I woke up, took two Xanax, and drove to work. All I remember is I hit my pillow, then I woke up and my arm hurt. When I walked out into the living room, my parents were staring at me, and all of the pills that used to be out in the kitchen were gone. I don't remember a fucking thing! But my parents told me what happened and it went down like this. Once I got to work, everybody thought I was drunk because I was stumbling over my feet and whenever anyone talked to me, I was just mumbling. It got bad and Will was worried. So he was gonna take me home, but I said I could just drive home. But he didn't let me, thank God he didn't. Once I got home, I went straight to my bed and flopped on it like a sack of potatoes being dropped on the ground. My mom came home 'cause Will called her. Once she got home, she was yelling my name but I wasn't responding. She and my uncle rushed me to the hospital and they basically had to drag me to the car and then drag me inside the hospital because I was just limp. Once I got there, my heartbeat and breathing were really slow. And once I finally came to, they had me pee in a cup, and that's when my parents found out about everything. It was a miracle that I even made it to work, let alone didn't die!

After they told me everything that happened, I didn't know what to say. I felt horrible, but I didn't know what to do. They finally asked me why I did it, and I think I said I didn't care about myself. It's not that I wanted to die. But I figured if I did die, it would make life easier, which is funny because if I died, there wouldn't be any life. I think the only reason I didn't take more was because I couldn't go without my friends and family. In my head, I didn't care if I died even though I definitely cared. I was just losing the battle against myself. I've never been crazy close to God. I mean, I talked to him a few times but not much. But after I almost died, I started talking to him a little more than I used to.

After the incident, we told everyone that it was exhaustion and that my body was so tired it was shutting down. I even told my friends that! Can you believe that shit!? I was so ashamed of myself that I couldn't even open up to some of the closest people in my life! So here I was, just my thoughts and me, no pills to try to avoid the problem. Instead, I had to take it head-on against my own mind.

The craziest thing to me is how lonely I felt even though I was surrounded by so many people who love me. On the outside, I was probably the happiest person in the world. But on the inside, it was very dark and scary. I felt so alone. I didn't want to talk to anybody because I didn't think it would help in any way. So I guess going to the hospital was actually for the best. All of the energy I was using to beat myself up and put myself down, I started putting into working out and making YouTube videos. If I slowed down at all, in my head I would call myself weak, not good enough, and basically all the things that you can think of. It would keep me going because I wasn't giving up. I didn't wanna lose to my thoughts and try and kill myself again. Of course, this is a lot easier said than done. But over a little while, it got a little better!

We were inching in on moving, and right before we moved, I had to get hernia surgery. I was told to not help with any of the boxes or other things while moving. I didn't listen and I helped. I was definitely hurting a little bit but nothing crazy. It was pretty bad because I wasn't the only person to have surgery that soon. Levi (my brother) just had surgery on his knee and my dad just had plates put in his neck so it's a family full of gimps doing shit they're not supposed to. So, the packing process was pretty fun, to say the least.

There were a lot of people I wanted to say bye to but I didn't have the time to go and see all of them so Kiara threw Dalton, Kade, and me a going-away party! The party was a blast. Most of the people I wanted to say goodbye to came but not all. As the night went on, Alyx kept looking at me and I got the vibe she was into me. We ended up going into a room and making out, but I wasn't that nice about it. While we were making out, I stopped and looked at her and said, "It's just like Kanye said!" She responded with "What!?" I then said the famous lyrics: "Wait a couple months then you gonna see, you'll never find nobody better than me." Which she wasn't too fond of but we kept making out. I was drunk and so was she, so there wasn't really any feeling behind it. Which is good because if I was sober, I would have been fucked because all of the feelings I used to have for her would have come back.

After the party, I rode home with Dalton. As we're driving, we talk about the party and look back on all the good times we had. Although we were very excited to be moving and doing something new, we were also very sad because the place we lived our entire lives we were finally going away from. I finally got home and stared up at my ceiling while in bed just embracing the fact that this is actually happening and to enjoy every moment no matter what.

After a couple days, it was time for us to move. Kade was meeting us at my house and Dalton was going with his family. We finished loading up all of the vehicles and it was now time to go! The drive was about eight hours but we were stopping in Pendleton because my parents had free rooms at the casino so it was gonna be cheaper. Then in the morning, we would finish the rest of our drive, which was about three hours.

We drove for about an hour and then we hit a rest area. We stopped because my dad had a freezer in the back seat of his truck full of a bunch of food and he wanted to make sure it was still on so the food inside didn't go bad. The freezer wasn't working so we had to lift it up and spin it around to reach a different outlet. This freezer is fucking heavy, and as we're picking it up, it lands on my hand, and then my dad spins it to turn it around. It cut my hand right open. Not the worst cut in the world but not good either. I couldn't stop bleeding so I had to get some gauze and bandages on it. Right when we were about to leave, Levi asked Kade if he could drive the Suburban because it used to be Levi's and he missed driving it. Kade didn't care so he rode with me for a long time. And the whole drive, my hand was hurting like a bitch. But it was OK because I was enjoying the drive.

After about five hours, we finally arrived in Pendleton. During the drive and the whole process, I was filming a video for YouTube, so once we got to Pendleton we messed around for a little bit and had fun with it. The thing about where we were staying was that it was a casino so we couldn't really screw around that much. But this place was nice. It had a bowling alley, movie theater, and an arcade, so Kade and I could do our own gambling, which I would say was more of just using your money as fire starter. Nonetheless, it was fun! My parents and Levi went to the casino and gambled for a little bit. While they did that, Kade and I got overpriced pizza that was really shitty, and then we kinda just did random things throughout the night. By about nine o'clock, we were all so wiped from the trip, we all fell asleep pretty fast. The next morning was the big day. It was the day we were officially moving in. We were leaving pretty early in the morning because we still had about a three-hour drive, and we didn't wanna get there when it was crazy busy. Once we got there, my parents and brother were shocked because they'd never seen the place in person, and overall, for the price, they thought it was a pretty nice place.

Getting everything into the apartment was a pain because, like I said, we're a family full of gimps besides my mom. Our apartment was upstairs, but once we got everything in, it was great! This apartment was actually the one we got a tour of when we first came and visited, so all of us were pretty happy about that. Only downside was our air conditioning wasn't working and it was super-hot. You could tell the people who get the apartment ready for the next people definitely rushed through it because it was a mess. Paint was everywhere and nothing was cleaned up. After we got all of our stuff in, everyone's family went to the store together to get things for our bathrooms and the living room, stuff like that. We all visited for the night because in the morning it was time for our families to go home. There's a place in Moscow called The Breakfast Club, and it has some of the most unique and delicious food you'll ever have. Dalton, Kade, and I went there when we visited, and I really wanted to go with my family. So, in the morning, we got up early so we could go before they left! The food was great, and they really enjoyed it. But now it was time for them to leave me for the first time in my twenty-year life.

It was hard for my dad and Levi, but my mom was the one having the hardest time with it. It didn't matter what I said to try and make it easier, because to her it wasn't going to get any easier. The way I looked at it was the longer I was to stay with my parents, the harder it was going to be. So the sooner you go on your own—of course, it's still going to be hard—but that will be when it's the easiest. My mom started to cry before they left and I saw my dad get teary-eyed. That's when I almost broke, but I didn't want a cry fest, so I kept my composure to hopefully help my mom and dad cry a little less. We all said our goodbyes, and just like that they were gone. I thought once I was left alone, I was going to break and just bawl my eyes out, but that never happened. It was a different experience because I was sad but I wasn't as sad as I was eager. Dalton was out doing stuff with his family, and as soon as he came back, he went straight to his room, and he didn't come out for a while. As soon as I saw that, I knew what was going on so I just let him be.

Now that we were on our own, the next step was for me to find a job because I wasn't gonna last forever on the money in my savings. Now, when it comes to jobs nowadays, everybody is hiring because every place needs people. But when it comes to if you want to do the work that's available, that's a different question. Most of the jobs that were hiring were jobs that I wasn't really interested in, like KFC, McDonald's, The Dollar Store, and so on. I wanted to try to find a job that paid pretty good money for what it was and something I didn't hate doing. The only problem with this was there was nothing out there that was calling my name. I decided to wait a little while and just focus on YouTube until something came up that I liked! While I was doing that, Kade was also looking for a job but wasn't having much luck, and Dalton was starting school soon, which he was excited about but also pretty damn nervous about. I mean, fair enough, I'm a huge people person but I would be shitting bricks. Even though Kade and I weren't going to school, all of us were dealing with that in our own way because now there were no parents around to help out. It was all on us to figure out what we were going to do and how we were gonna do it. About a month went by and I still didn't have a job, which sucked, but I was really going hard on YouTube. I just wasn't making money from it, so it was becoming kind of an issue, but I wasn't stressed about it. One thing about moving is back home we had our friends who we would go hang out with, but here, it was just us. We only knew each other, which was fine, but we needed to meet new people.

All of us like Elvis, but out of everyone I know, Dalton is his biggest fan. I mean, the dude knows everything about him. If you have a question, he most likely has the answer. One night, we were all hanging out doing our own thing in our rooms. I got done with whatever I was doing in my room. So I went over to Dalton's room and that's when I found Elvis sunglasses. I thought they were sick, so I put them on and started fucking around. Then Dalton put them on and we started singing "Jailhouse Rock" loudly and imitating Elvis's dance moves all the way into Kade's room. By no means were we being quiet, and just as we started back up singing, we heard a knock at the door. You would have thought there was gunfire coming toward us. All of us hid, and it got really quiet, literally a hundred to zero. Nobody wanted to answer the door because we thought someone was really pissed at us. We couldn't hide forever, so I opened the door and that's when I saw.

CHAPTER 12

New Friends and Love

As I opened the door, nobody was there, but out of the corner of my eye, I saw something fall. All of us looking at each other confused, we picked up what fell. It was a note folded in half and inside it said: "If you wanna hang out, you're under 25 and not creepy, check yes or no!" We all laughed at the note, intrigued but also baffled. On the note, we checked yes, and I left my phone number on it so they could get a hold of us easier. On the note in small letters, it said leave at the bottom of the stairs, sooo that's what we did. After about five minutes, I get a phone call. When I answer, it's a girl talking, and you can tell we're both hesitant to say the next thing. She then asks us if we wanna come downstairs to hang out, and, of course, without even thinking about it, we said yes. As soon as we got downstairs, you could tell there was this awkward kinda tension, which makes sense based on the fact that this was our first time meeting new people. The nice thing about all of it was they were drinking, so everybody had a little buzz, which I feel like made it a lot easier for everyone to talk to one another. There were three girls living downstairs—Alivia, Bella, and Jaelyn—and then there was a guy down there who was Alivia's boyfriend and his name was Gavin. All of us kinda clicked pretty fast. Of course, like I said, it was a little awkward and we didn't go out of our way too much, but after being there for about ten minutes, it was great! All of us started visiting and getting to know each other. It was like we'd known each other for years!

As we were all hanging out, I heard a loud bang on the apartment window followed by some laughing. All of us looked at each other wondering who it was. Then Bella jumped up to go get the door, and it was her friend Alexis with some guy named Wyatt. As soon as I saw her, I couldn't take my eyes off her. As we meet, she's definitely drunk, and I guess that night was her twenty-first birthday, so kind of a funny time to meet somebody. For the rest of the time she was there, I kept looking at her, and then I would look at the guy, curious as to if they were dating or just friends and comparing me to him as if I was dating her. I was almost annoying myself wondering if she was dating this guy. After a little while, they left. It was getting pretty late so we headed back up the stairs.

Once we got back into our apartment, Dalton goes, "Holy hell, did you see Bella's friend!?" I then responded, "Hell yeah, I couldn't stop looking at her!!" We talked about the night for a while and how all of us were excited that we met some new friends. After talking with Dalton for a little while, I said, "I'm gonna try and date Bella's friend." He responded with a "good luck" followed by a laugh, and then everybody went to bed.

Days went on and I was still going strong with YouTube but I was running out of money and needed to find a job fast. I kept looking and nothing was catching my eye until I saw a server job at Buffalo Wild Wings. Now, I have never been a server in my life, but I loved people and everybody always told me I'd be good at it, so I thought, why not?! I applied for it and within the day I got a phone call back. They wanted me to come in for an interview ASAP, so I dressed kinda nice and went in. As soon as I was done with the first two questions, I knew I had the job. But then he asked me if I ever had any experience as a server, and when I told him no, he wasn't the biggest fan. They still needed a lot of positions so he asked if I wanted to be a host. Overall, I didn't, but he said in about two weeks he would move me up to a server. I needed a job so I didn't really give a shit. He also told me he was hiring cooks and if I referred a friend I would make some money. So I told Kade about the job and he ended up getting an interview a couple days later. I started work in about a week. In the meantime, I was just hanging out and staying on the YouTube grind.

Kiara would come up and visit Kade, and pretty soon she was moving in with us. So all of us were figuring our own things out. One day, all of us went to Target, and while going up and down the aisles, we found ourselves in the board game section. We had been wanting to get some sort of game but weren't quite sure which one. As we were looking, we came across this card game called Stir the Pot. The concept of this game was you draw a card and only you and the person to your left can see it. Once you see the card, you then have to point at somebody who best fits the card. After you point at the person, there is a coin you flip that says tell or don't tell. Based on what it lands on, you'll either have to tell the person what the card said or you won't. Now you see why it's called Stir the Pot 'cause, oh man, people get pissed. So, we really wanted it! One night, Bella invited us down to hang out with her and Alexis. Kade didn't end up going 'cause I think he was hanging with Kiara. Dalton and I, of course, said yes, and we brought down Stir the Pot. Once we got downstairs, we started drinking a little bit and visiting, and I'd say after about fifteen minutes, everybody wanted to play the game. The big thing with this game with Bella and Alexis was that we didn't know them, so we were literally judging a book by its cover. That's messed up, but overall, that's what everyone was doing because nobody knew one another except I knew Dalton and Bella knew Alexis.

I was really looking forward to Alexis's answers because even though this was only the second time I'd ever seen this girl, I had a huge crush on her! I just couldn't get her face out of my head. As we were playing the game, everyone's laughing and having a good time. But some of her answers are going toward me and then some are going toward Dalton, and she's like eyeballing both of us. I'm so fucking confused! I don't have a clue who she's into, and to be honest, she might not like either of us and just have a flirtatious personality. All I know is that I didn't know anything. I think I was just picturing her liking me in my head, hoping it was real. As we keep playing the game, we look at the clock and it's six thirty in the morning! We've been up the whole night and nobody even noticed 'cause we were having so much fun playing the game. All of us were going to head to bed, but we realized The Breakfast Club opened up at seven so we forced ourselves to stay up so we could go get breakfast together.

Breakfast was great and the whole time I couldn't keep my eyes off of Alexis. But once again, it was stupid because I didn't know what she was feeling. Usually, I'm the type of guy to just go after it if I want it, but once we got back to the apartment, I told Dalton I wasn't going to do anything.

She was going to have to make the move toward one of us if she wanted anything. We both made an agreement to not do anything or try to make a move until we both knew who she liked or if she even liked one of us. Once we had that conversation, I hit the pillow hard 'cause I hadn't slept all night. The main thing I also kept thinking about was quitting Buffalo Wild Wings. I was making shitty money, and I was still a host after about a month so I was about done. Basically, I just didn't go in. When they called, I told them I wasn't scheduled and that I was looking for other jobs. So, I told them thank you but I think I'll be moving on. Now I know that's not a good way of doing it, but shit, who cares? It's not like it was gonna go on my résumé anyway. I was only a host, so who cares?!

It's great that I was done with that job. But now it was back to job searching, which was such a pain in the ass because most of the jobs were not paying very much or it was back to the same thing before. A bunch of shit I don't want to do! I was staying pretty consistent on the YouTube grind. I mean, of course, every now and then I would slip up, but for the most part I was solid. Dalton and I were hanging out one night and from the last time we hung out with Alexis and Bella, we got their Snapchats. So, while we were hanging out, I got a random snap from Alexis. As soon as I saw it, I lit up! The snap said, "Hey, I got a bottle of wine and there's a show I wanna watch. You wanna hang out and help me finish it?" I've only had wine one time in my life and I thought it tasted like piss! Buuttt I really wanted to hang out with her, so I jumped on the opportunity and said, "Hell, yeah!" On her way over, I was so hyped up! Of course, I still didn't know if she liked me, but Dalton was pretty sure she did. But in my book, maybe she just wanted to hang out even though I was hoping something would happen. Once she got to the apartment, she was wearing the same off-white McCall, Idaho, hoodie from the first night we met her and some spandex shorts that the hoodie was hanging over, with glasses. I didn't know she wore glasses, but when I asked her about them, she just said they were like a blue-light pair of glasses so it's not as stressful on her eyes. She was perfect from head to toe, and I couldn't stop myself from freezing up around her.

She poured herself a glass of wine and then one for me. I took a drink and did the best acting job of a lifetime to not say it tasted like shit. Instead, I said, "That's not too bad!" After the wine was poured, Dalton, Alexis, and I then started watching this new Netflix show about how there are two twin sisters but they each live each other's life. Yeah, I know, it's really confusing. Overall, I liked the show, but the thing is, I don't sit down and watch TV very much. The only time I do is if it's a movie or something like that. I liked the show, but I was kinda done with it and wanted to do something else. But I knew she wanted to watch it, and I really didn't want her to leave so all of us continued watching it. The way we were sitting on the couch was Alexis in the middle, Dalton on her left, and I was on her right. As we're all watching the show, I see Alexis's hand on the couch in a way that says, "Hey, hold my hand." But I'm terrified, so instead of just going for it, I put my hand on the couch right next to hers. As my hand gets closer to hers, I can feel my breathing slow down but my heart pumping faster. Then, finally my finger touches her finger! *Wow, do I sound like a pussy!* I don't know what's going on. Usually, I can just go for it, but with her, I'm terrified, so I'm just trying to play my cards right! After that stellar move I just made,

Dalton then got up and left to go play basketball, which he didn't really care about doing, but he was leaving me with her, which was nice of him. Once he left, it was still close to the same thing, but I got a little closer to her. Then, finally we were actually holding hands even though it felt like a sauna in my hands because of how nervous I was. It didn't matter because I was ecstatic and she was too! After about another hour or two of watching the show, she was getting up to head home. I walked her to the door happy but also sad because she was now leaving. Once I opened the door for her, she said, "Thank you! Tonight was really fun." I, of course, agreed, and right when she was about to leave, she grabbed my shirt and pulled me in for a kiss. You know when you're a kid and you ask to go to McDonald's and your mom always says no but then one day out of nowhere she finally says yes!? Well, that's what this kiss felt like. Her lips were so soft, and the way she looked at me made me melt! I've never felt anything like that. I felt like I was floating and was the happiest I'd ever been. As soon as she was out the door, I jumped in joy and told Dalton what happened and texted her almost immediately!

The next day, we kept texting, and the next, and so on and so on. Bella and she were going to some rodeo in Lewiston, which is about forty-five minutes from us, and they asked if Dalton and I wanted to go. We were really excited to go because it was the first time we were leaving Moscow to do something different, which is funny to say because everything we were doing was new. Dalton and I were trying to dress a little nice for the rodeo, and when Bella and Alexis came to pick us up, it didn't matter what I looked like, my jaw dropped again! She was wearing short jean shorts, a white T-shirt, and a flannel that was this light brown. I couldn't keep my eyes off of her, and the whole time I'm thinking to myself, I'm one lucky son of a bitch. The rodeo was a lot of fun, and then we came back to the apartment, and she spent the night. We were kissing each other and feeling on each other all night, and I was sooo happy. Now, don't say, "Oh well, that's because you're a guy and she's a girl," 'cause that's not it!! I was obsessed with this girl. I've made out with people in the past and haven't liked it that much, but this had something in it, she was like a drug and I didn't wanna stop taking her.

    I was still job searching from day to day and wasn't finding too much of anything that piqued my interest, but at the same time, Alexis and I were talking every day so it made everything better. Later that night, she was at a party and asked for a ride, and that's when I met Brody. Now, as soon as I met him, I knew he was a nice guy and he was really funny. He was just one of those people who are down to earth and you didn't need to know too much about them to tell they are a good person. After a little bit of talking among the four of us—Dalton was there too—I got invited to a frat party, which overall was pretty impossible for me to get into because: 1.) I'm a guy and they don't want more guys at the party because then girls might not focus on them; and 2.) This is the big one, I didn't even go to school, so for them to let me in was going to be slim to none, but shit, I mean it was worth a shot! After a few more days, it was Friday and it was time for the party! Alexis and I were practically already dating, but we weren't official so I was planning on doing it tonight or tomorrow. We went to Brody's frat first to pregame before we went to the party. Brody's frat was Lambda, and the guys in that house are some of the nicest people I've met! They let me in with open arms and treated me with respect. We went upstairs to Brody's room, which is where I met his girlfriend, Amaya. Amaya and Alexis were roommates in their sorority and best friends. After a few games and drinks, it was time to go to the party, which I surprisingly got into really easily. I guess a big part is who you know, and Brody knew a good chunk of people. And the other part is confidence. I walked everywhere with my head high, so for me, that wasn't a problem.

Once we were in, it was packed! I loved every second of it. Of course, as usual, Alexis looked super good, and we were dancing with each other, and we had alcohol in our systems, which can be a good or bad thing, but in this case, it was a great thing! As we're dancing, Alexis pulls me close and says in my ear, "I love you." I stopped and said, "Wait, what did you just say!?" Of course, I knew what she said, but I wanted to see if she would say it again. She then got shy and said, "Oh, it was nothing." I've been told "I love you" before and I've said it back because I didn't want to be a dick. But I honestly knew I was in love with her, and I only knew her for a couple weeks! I grabbed her face and yelled over the blaring music, "Alexis, I love you too!!" We then kissed each other to seal what we just said and then we made it official!

Dalton came and picked up Alexis and me and we went back to the apartment. (Note to Mom: go ahead and skip this part!) We had sex that night, and it was the greatest sex of my life, which wasn't a big shock because I hadn't had a lot of it. But with the way I felt about her, my love grew even stronger. I know a lot of people might think it's too early to be in love, but I don't think you can put a time on it. Love is love, and that's just how it works! The morning we woke up, I rolled over and saw her and my heart just filled up with joy! I knew we had something special!

I was keeping up on YouTube pretty regularly and the channel was growing! Not millions, but everything's a milestone! I then found a job landscaping, which I didn't really wanna do too much, but it paid me money and I needed a job because it was important. But now I had a girlfriend, and they aren't cheap, so I wanted to do everything I could to make her happy too!

I worked at that job for a month and said, "Fuck that!" It was shitty work that didn't pay enough and I wasn't about to do something I hated waking up in the morning to go do. After about a week, I went to a gym downtown and dropped off a résumé. The girl working at the front desk put mine on top for some reason, and then boom, the next day, I was hired! It was a job and it was at a gym. I mean, for me, I was in heaven!

Bella invited all of us out to her grandma's cabin, so Dalton, Alexis, and I all went. This place was beautiful. When I first met Bella, I knew she had money, but God damn! She had a lot of money. This was one of the nicest if not the nicest cabin I'd been in, and I was there with the girl of my dreams, which made it even better!! Now I have a job, a girlfriend, and life's great. So I'm gonna skip through a lot of the dates and everything else because it's just repetitive for all of you guys! But what I will say is there was a lot of sex…like a lot, laughs, cries, and some of the best moments with my friends!

Things were going great and then tragedy struck in Moscow, Idaho. Four kids were killed in their sleep right down the road from the university. Of course, this struck panic into everyone. They shut down school, and people were leaving way earlier than expected. We were all heading home for the holidays anyway, but for some people, it was a lot earlier. Alexis went home, but I still had about a week before I left for about a week or two.

Once I was back home, I got her a couple Christmas gifts. One of the gifts was a green and white pair of Air Force 1s and the other was a diamond rose-gold bracelet. Did I have the money for it? Fuck no! But I really wanted to get her something special because I loved her! Christmas back home was great! It was really nice to see the family and we all shared a lot of laughs. It was closing in on New Year's Eve and I really wanted to spend New Year's with Alexis, but her parents wouldn't let her come back to Moscow until the murderer was found and everything was resolved. She was gonna go out that night with some friends in Boise, which really sucked because I wanted to be there with her, but I was happy she was having a good time! I was already back in Moscow but with my family 'cause they came back up with me, so we spent the New Year's together until they went to bed. Then it was just me drinking 5 percent Arnold Palmers and playing Madden 23. I really missed Alexis, so we ended up talking for most of the night because her plans fell through, which sucked. But to an extent, I was happy because Alexis was a very attractive person. She would dress really nice out so I was never a fan of her going out to the bars or the frat parties alone, but I trusted her so it was no big deal! Talking with her that night made me so happy because I hadn't seen her for a couple weeks, which might not seem like much, but we were spending every day with each other beforehand, so it was hard.

About a month went by and I still hadn't seen Alexis. So we talked about it, and I was going to take a flight up to Boise! The only scary part was it was my first flight in my entire life and I was doing it alone!! I was *terrified*!! But I didn't wanna go another day without seeing her so we split the plane ticket. I brought the presents I got her and hopped on a flight to Boise! Thankfully, there were some really nice people in line and on the plane to help me through the whole thing, and before you know it, we were landing.

Once I got to the Boise airport, I was lost, so I called Alexis who was waiting out front and she guided the way. I stepped out and there she was! A white and gray flannel, her skin glowing with her dark black curled hair, and her eyes that made me melt, all looked at me at once as I gave her the biggest kiss I could imagine. I wasn't back in my hometown but being with her felt like home! We stopped by a place and got some food for when we got to her place because I didn't get in until about 10:00 p.m. Finally, we got to her house, and it was a really nice place, big backyard, super nice bright-white kitchen. There was a downstairs area where her and her brother Ashton's rooms were at. Ashton was the only one up, so I got to meet him and we instantly clicked. He was a good kid, but I'm also pretty sure he was like that with everybody because that's just the kind of person he was. After I scarfed down the burger I got, I wanted to finally give Alexis her gifts. We exchanged and she loved hers, which, I mean, like duh, of course! Why wouldn't she like it!? Then I got mine, and she felt bad because they weren't as expensive as mine, but shit, I never cared about that kind of stuff. Just the fact that somebody would go out of their way and get me something was more than enough for me! As I opened the gift bag, there was a bunch of different stuff— cologne, body wash, a coffee cup that said "You're My Favorite." But out of all of these things, the last thing I saw was a Christmas ornament. On the bottom of the ornament, it said "Hunter and Alexis 2023."

Then she looked at me and said, "It'll be our first of many as we get older." That was the best gift in the world I could have gotten because it really showed that it wasn't just me but both of us were in this for the long run!

(Also, before I go any further, I kinda messed up the timeline here. I went over to her place before Christmas and then she stayed there till a little after New Year's. Soooo, now that we're all caught up, let's get back to it!)

The next morning, I got to meet her parents. I was a little excited, but to an extent shitting bricks, because I was a guy who wasn't in college and my overall dream was to do YouTube. Let's just say they frowned upon that, but Alexis said she didn't care and it didn't matter what they thought because she was happy. I greeted them with handshakes, and then Alexis, her dad, and I went to the store to pick up some stuff. They were up front having conversations the whole time about a bunch of people and things that I didn't know about, but whenever I saw the opportunity, I would try to join in to show both of them that I cared what they were talking about. We got back to the house and I went and hung out with Alexis and her brother. After a while, we went to the coffee shop she used to work at and got a drink together. Also, that was her thing, she loved coffee whether it was drinking it or making it. It was one of her passions, and one day she wanted to open a shop of her own. I thought that was a really cool thing to wanna do. But shit, who am I kidding, she could have wanted to be a yo-yoer and I would've been all for it.

When we got back, it was time for dinner, and her dad was making burgers for everyone. While he was cooking dinner, Ashton, Alexis, and I were playing a board game and having some drinks. This was the time I felt like I was starting to grow on the family, and they were starting to like me because I was a straight shooter. What you see is what you get, and I'm not going to change myself for anybody. Overall, I think they respected that, and they respected the way I treated Alexis. I spent a few more days there and met some more of her family, which I really enjoyed. I saw myself going back there, no question. If Alexis ever wanted me there, I'd hop on a plane without hesitation. But now it was time for me to go back, which was shitty, but I felt like our love grew even stronger with what the situation was.

After what felt like years, she was finally back. Around this time, it was getting close to my twenty-first birthday. I celebrated with everybody except Dalton, who couldn't go to the bars. So, when I got back, all of us smoked some cigars and drank a little bit before I crashed and went to bed. The thing I was most excited about was going to my hometown with Alexis this time. My whole family knew how crazy I was about her, and I talked very highly of her, so they were really excited to meet her. Once we got into Oregon, we went to my house, and from there, we were going to the coast to a casino called Three Rivers because now I was finally old enough to lose money! As soon as she met my family, I fell in love with the idea of this being a regular thing one day for the both of us and for both of our families. The way that everyone talked to each other, you could tell they truly cared about what the person was saying and they liked one another. Once we got to the casino, my family kept telling me: "Yes Hunter, we love her. She's the one for you!" The whole time I was back home with her, I enjoyed every second of it and couldn't have pictured anything better. We couldn't stay for too long, just about a weekend, but that was more than enough to realize even more how much I truly loved this person.

While hanging with Alexis every day, I was also hanging out with Brody, Amaya, and Maggie a lot more. Maggie was another one of Alexis's roommates, and she was one of the sweetest people I've met. We were all hanging out a lot more so we decided to plan a trip out by Coeur d'Alene. It was such a beautiful place. All of us were going to snowboard and ski while we were there because it was packed with snow. The trip was a ton of fun, and I got to know even more about all of them, and I became closer than I was before. They were all really good people, and I would call them my close friends.

While we were on that trip, I learned some stuff about Alexis, though, that just kinda shocked me because I didn't know why she would tell me. All of us were drinking, and she said her body count number—the number of people she's had sex with—I think that number was around forty. When I said, "*Huh!?*," she said, "Oh, nothing!" The thing is, I knew she had sex with a lot of people, I just didn't know it was that many. I mean, I didn't care because she was with me, and she wasn't that same person that she used to be. It was just a number, and to me, it didn't matter because we loved one another.

The only other thing I heard about her was from Brody. Alexis and Amaya went to bed, so Brody, Maggie, and I stayed up and talked about a bunch of stuff. Brody told me that when he first met me, he didn't want Alexis to date me because he was scared she was gonna ruin me. Her ex cheated on her, and then she went out and cheated back, and I guess he just wasn't a big fan of hers. As we started hanging out with everyone, he could see that she changed with me so he started to really like her. Once again, I was a little shocked, but I was mostly just shocked that she didn't tell me any of it. I never brought it up to her, and after that talk, it never was a thought of mine.

After that trip, we came back and I was invited to hang out at Miranda and Bailey's apartment with everyone. Miranda was Amaya's sister, and Bailey was Miranda's boyfriend. The reason we started hanging out over there was because Brody was taking a break from school and staying over there, so we would go chill with all of them. I'm just bringing this up so you know more names but once again also very good people!

CHAPTER 13

Sadness and Anger

Alexis and I were falling in love more and more every day and things were moving fast. Graduation was right around the corner, and she got a job offer from Sherwin Williams in Spokane Valley, which was about an hour and a half from Moscow. We were talking about some of the next steps in our relationship and maybe getting a place together. I mean, yeah, it was really early, but I didn't oppose the idea. I mean, I wanted to marry her one day so we went together to look at apartments.

Once we got up there, some of the ones she had picked out were really bad, and we didn't even go inside to check them out because the area was really sketchy. But after a few more, we found one that was beautiful! It had its own gym, hot tub, and movie theater. The place was really clean, and on top of that, the price split between two people wasn't bad. On her own, it would be too much, but if we did actually move in together, it was perfect. After looking at the apartments together we went around Spokane a little bit, and the thoughts running through both of our heads were crazy. We both were on board with doing it. Of course, we didn't pull the trigger or anything yet, but the thought was real and becoming even more real because it was getting close. Alexis talked with her stepmom Erica and she thought it was too early, but so did we. We didn't really care because we loved each other so much, and this was the next step in our journey! I started looking for jobs around the area.

After a little while, I was feeling a little homesick so I decided to go back home. I really wanted Alexis to come with me, but she had a lot going on with school because graduation was coming up and she was working a lot to try to stack some cash for after graduation. I was going home for a week, and it was just like any other time. But about midway through the week, Alexis came up with a decision and said that she thought it was too early to move in with each other. I told her that it takes both of us to be fully in it, so it's not a big deal. Then, she asked me to come home because one of the frats was throwing a party and it was parents weekend. But I wanted to spend the rest of the week with the family, which I could tell made her a little upset. That made me upset, but we talked about it and we were fine! She sent me pics of her at the party having fun the next day.

Here's the thing: Alexis and I have gotten in arguments in the past. During one of them, she said that YouTube's just a hobby and that I wasn't doing anything with my life. That was after a party she went to, so she was a little drunk. I thought we were going to break up that day, but we got over that bump in the road. The other big argument we got into was about her going to frat parties alone because when she would go, she dressed real sexy, and guys would hit on her all the time. I trusted her, but I didn't trust the guys because they could give a fuck about me. That argument ended with her yelling at me, calling me an asshole, and that I was overreacting. She said she was just having fun with her friends. To myself, I thought, you know what, she's right, maybe I was overreacting. After that, I didn't care anymore because I trusted her with everything I had. So, when she sent me those pictures, I got a little upset because of the situation and the fact that she was trying to make me feel a little bad for missing the party. I did feel bad about it, and I was pissed, but I was just glad she had fun.

Once I got back to Moscow, it was so great to be with her again. I felt warm and not worried about anything in the world. She always made me feel like that. Our six months passed and we didn't even realize it so we wanted to celebrate it together. But we had to find time for later down the road because we were both busy. Once I came back, it was really busy because her sorority, Theta, had a poker night coming up and a formal dance. I went out with Alexis and got some nicer clothes because the next day was poker night. I know this sounds like a lot, but it was literally within the week I got back this happened, and then the next week was the formal.

Alexis and I went to dinner before we went over to Miranda and Bailey's apartment because we were gonna pregame a little before the poker night. She was stunning! She wore this shiny red dress that was tighter around her waist and looser up top, and she was the walking definition of one in a million. Dinner was great and so was the pregame, but poker night was shit! There were supposed to be dealers with all of the tables set up with different games. Instead, not a single table was set up, and we just had to play our own game if we wanted to play any games. We stayed there for no longer than twenty minutes. We then went back to the apartment, had a lot of laughs, drinks, and food, and we all turned a shitty night into a great one!

The next week while I was at work, I met this guy named Spencer. He always came into the gym, but we never talked to one another. One day before I was about to leave, we got into a conversation about video games, YouTube, the Moscow area, and what both of our plans were. I felt like we were instant friends. We got each other's Snapchats, and then boom, I met another person in Moscow who I could now hang out with.

Now, coming up was the formal dance. I went shopping and got new clothes again because I really wanted to look good for her. It's not that I thought I looked horrible at the poker night, but I wanted to try to look great for her. She was once again—no shock to anybody—*drop-dead stunning*!! This time, she wore a shorter black dress that had little glimmers of stars. Everything about her was incredible. We stopped by the liquor store beforehand because we were gonna sneak in the drinks. We got in fine and went to the bathroom to drink a little. When we came out, we were dancing with everyone. Then, the girls went to the bathroom and one of them got caught with a vape, so we ended up leaving early. That really sucked because I loved dances, and I loved dancing with Alexis even more. But once again, we went back to Miranda and Bailey's place and made up for another ruined Theta event.

The next week, Brody and Ruben were coming in from Oregon. We were all super stoked to hang out, and I was looking forward to Alexis meeting Ruben. She had already met Brody. We were all going out to the shops around downtown Moscow and then other places to eat to show Brody and Ruben around. One of the nights we were going to throw a party and have everyone over! We invited our old downstairs neighbor. Alexis, of course, was coming with

Brody and all of them. They just took a little bit to make it over. But the party was set and it was great!

Alexis walked in and I was stunned. Honestly, I felt like I fell in love with her all over again. Seriously, I didn't think anything could be as great and look as great as she did, and I was right until I saw her that night. Everybody met each other, and usually I would have been all over Alexis and just focus on her. But we had a lot of people over and our close friends from Oregon so I wasn't just focused on her. That was fine, but the only thing was she was off the whole party. I didn't know what it was, but I could tell something wasn't right, and it gave me a weird feeling. As the night went on, people started to head out, and Alexis went to bed. She wanted me to join her, but my friends were over so I told her I'd hop in later and gave her a kiss. As the night was coming to an end and almost everybody was gone, I texted Spencer and asked if he wanted to come over. It took a little bit but he came over with about six other people, which wasn't a problem to me because the more the merrier, and it was one hell of a night! Everyone was having a good time, all of my friends liked Spencer and his friends, and I couldn't have asked for a better night. I just wish Alexis could have met all of them. They all left at about 2:00 in the morning so I don't blame her for being clocked out because I was about to pass out myself. I thanked Spencer and everybody else for coming out before I went to bed. As I hopped into bed, I wrapped my arms around the warm beauty that I got to call mine, but she didn't seem too happy. So I stopped, but then she made a noise and pulled me closer to her. She did it a lot because when she's tired, she gets grouchy, and I always thought it was the cutest thing. So I had a smile from ear to ear with a warm heart as I fell asleep.

The next morning, Alexis had to work, so we talked for a little before she left. Everything seemed fine, so as I would usually do, I gave her a kiss, told her I loved her, and then she was off. All of the boys got up and went out to breakfast before they all left the next day. We wanted to take them out to The Breakfast Club because it had some of the best and most unique breakfasts in town. It was a really good morning!

Later in the night, all of us filmed a video together for YouTube, which brought back old times and it was a lot of fun. During the day, Alexis was hanging out at some fire with a frat and some of her friends so I didn't wanna bug her. Graduation was coming up soon for her so she needed to get as much time with her friends as possible. She didn't stay the night that night of the video. The next morning, I texted her and asked if we were OK. I walked out into the living room and talked with the guys, and that's when I got a text back from her that said, "I think we should talk." My heart sank, and I looked at the guys and said, "Well, I think I'm getting dumped today." All of them were shocked, they asked why, and I told them I had no idea.

But now I understood why she was acting weird those last couple of days. I wanted to see her that day, but she was at a fire again with a frat, and she said she just wanted to talk later that night. Brody and Ruben were now gone, and the whole day I was eating myself alive waiting for this conversation. That text is never good. Out of everything in the world, those are the five words I hate. She was finally ready to be picked up, and I took some deep breaths and prepared myself before I walked out the door and texted her that I was on my way.

Once I got to Theta to pick her up, she looked upset. As she got in the car, we didn't hug or kiss, and right at that moment, I knew I was fucked. We went to a place she showed me when we first started talking called the Top of the World. It has a view of the entire city, which isn't much, but man, was it pretty.

She started talking to me, and I wanted to look at her. But as she was talking, I was mostly looking straight ahead as I bit the inside of my cheeks thinking about all of the plans we were talking about and how they were all getting burned in this conversation. We kept talking for a while. The reason Alyx dumped me was because she wanted to try new things in the future, and this was the same thing but from a different mouth this time. She looked at me and said, "I just think we're both in different parts of our lives and neither of us knows what the future holds and you don't have life figured out right now." We had this same conversation about four months ago so I didn't understand what the real reason was, but she said that that was it.

I was just shocked because literally a week ago, we were looking into each other's eyes telling one another "I love you" and "I'm gonna marry you," and within a week it gets thrown out the window!? Then the month before that, we were literally talking about living with each other! I was so lost, and that's when I started to cry. I couldn't look at her while I was crying because I would've cried even harder. I was just thinking about everything we did and how it was all just through within a few words that shot through my heart like a knife. She was crying most of the time, which I never understood. I mean, why are you crying if you're the one dealing the hand? I told her she was only moving an hour away and asked if she at least wanted to try it. She said no, and I wasn't the one to beg, so that was it! The girl I thought I was gonna do everything with—marry, have a family, grow old together, ya know, some *Notebook* shit—and just like that, it was all over.

I got home and told everybody, and they all just kinda looked at me and didn't say much. I wanted to cry more, but now I felt so dead in my mind and my heart that I couldn't force tears out even if I wanted to. I was a literal zombie. I told everybody that I was gonna go to the gym. Once I got there, I just sat at the machine looking at old pictures, typing texts to her, and deleting them before I sent them. After about fifteen minutes, Dalton came into the gym and asked how I was doing. He knew I was far from good, but he wanted to check up on me. He told me he never really saw us going very far with each other because we were two very different people. He also knew I wasn't happy, so he didn't say much. Of course, talking with my best friend or just being around him helped. But I was still so dead that my answers were bland, and he knew it, so he left me to hit my workout. The night was rough, but I ended up falling asleep decently because I was so mentally tired.

The next day I got a call from my mom who told me that our childhood dog, Tika, had passed away, which really hurt. But I was already so broken that it was hard to cry. I knew Alexis really liked Tika, so I texted her just to let her know what happened. She texted me back and said, "omg I'm so sorry how are you doing?" I texted her back, and she didn't text me back for six hours. So I deleted the text 'cause I figured she didn't really care 'cause she never got back to me. She was at the frats again at a fire so that explained why she never texted me back.

Spencer was texting me about coming out to the bars because it was his friend's twenty-first birthday. Her name was Kendall and I only met her once before. It was at my apartment. She was one of the people who came with him. I was gonna stay home that night and just sulk, which I know isn't good for me. But I was pretty sad about the situation, so I didn't really wanna go out. Dalton thought it was a good idea for me to go out because he knows I love people and being around them would be a good thing for me. I kinda argued back, but I didn't have an argument, so I ended up meeting them at one of the bars.

The night was actually really great. I was getting to know everybody more and I was actually laughing. If I wasn't laughing, something was wrong, so it felt nice to kinda be back for a bit. That feeling lasted for about the first hour when we were at the first bar. We walked a little down the road to a bar called Mingles. Out of all the bars, Mingles had the best prices and pool tables, so we were looking forward to it.

We walked in, and as I gave the bouncer my ID, it was the first time in my life I became completely paralyzed and wanted to cry on the spot. It felt as if my soul left my body, and I couldn't say anything. I was stuttering and just pointing in the direction as everybody asked me what was wrong. This was the very next day, and there I saw Alexis all over a guy like she used to be all over me, his hand on her ass, her laughing, holding hands, she even kissed him. Now, I know this might sound fucked to you guys, but in my book, if you looked at somebody and told them you loved them and were gonna marry them and then the next day, you do some shit like that!? You never loved them in the first place!

We continued into the bar, and I did my best to ignore her and the guys she was with. Oh yeah, guess what? They were frat guys, which I never had any beef with, but it was one of the ones at the fires she was going to, which made my heart sink even more. We got a table and I did my best to keep my happy face on. I told everyone what was going on, and, of course, they were doing their best to support me. But really, the only thing that was remotely helping was drinking more with them 'cause I could focus on not throwing up rather than focus on her.

She looked really good. Her hair was all done up, and she was wearing close to the same outfit she was when she came over to the apartment for the party. I didn't wanna look at her, but I was still in love with her, so it was pretty hard to just stop on a dime and focus on other people. We got a pool table, and while we were playing, she was walking straight toward me because the group she was with was right behind us. We made eye contact, and then she just looked down and walked right past me as if I was a stranger. My heart sank to my stomach as the smile I had toward her faded away and turned to sadness.

I saw her talk to all the guys she was with as they looked in my direction and then she grabbed the one she was all over. She grabbed both of his hands and put them on her shoulders as she walked out of the bar smiling. The way they looked together, you would have thought they'd been together for months! Then I started talking to myself in my head and got even more sad, but now I was pissed! I was saying to myself: "That motherfucker doesn't have shit on you, he's not even close! Why the *fuck* would she pick him!!" Then I started getting mad at her and was wondering why she would do such an awful thing! But that anger then turned to sadness, and I told all of them that I was gonna leave because I was just being a downer and I didn't really wanna be out anymore. They all hyped me up in the best way they could, and I stayed for the rest of the night! They were the ones who helped me that night, and although I was eating myself alive, they helped me through it! Once I got home, I laid in bed till about four in the morning just thinking. I still couldn't cry because I was so tired. I mean, my body wanted to, but I wouldn't let it.

The next morning, I texted Maggie, Amaya, and Brody and told them what I saw and how I was feeling. All of them texted me back saying how fucked up that was. That's when the shit hit the fan. Maggie texted me and told me things that she thought I should know. At this point, I was feeling like I wasn't good enough for her, which was far from true. But with how we broke up, I didn't know why and I was so confused.

Maggie knew that's how I was feeling, and told me the truth but only the beginning of it. She told me about two months into the relationship, she was always texting other guys. And at one of our formals while we were together, she asked somebody else to go with her, but the guys said no because she had a boyfriend. Once I found this out, I was pissed and hurt ten times worse than before. But just when I thought it was horrible, it was just the beginning.

Amaya and Maggie talked to me about the big one. Little did I know it was about to send me into a pool of deep, dark shit that was gonna be hard to get out of. Amaya said that when I went to Oregon the second time—ya know, the time she was mad at me because she wanted me to go out the frats—well, holy fuck, did she get her revenge. I met with all of them so we could talk about it even more in person to understand it a little better instead of just texting back and forth or calling.

I was now at Miranda and Bailey's apartment with everybody there. We were gonna talk about it a little, but they were gonna do their best to soften the blow. Not Brody.

He said I deserved the right to know everything, and so, Maggie and Amaya told me everything. It all started on one of the nights I was gone. They knew that she texted other guys and was touchy with people at the frats, which to an extent pissed me off that they never told me. But Alexis was their best friend, so I don't blame them for not ratting out on her. But if Brody knew, it would have been a different story. Anyway, back to the big one. One of the nights I was gone all of them were hanging out and they were gonna go to GrubTruck, which is a mac-and-cheese truck downtown. All of them were up for it except Alexis because she wasn't feeling too hot and said she was gonna go to bed, so they said no worries and went anyway.

The next morning, they all got a text from Alexis saying how she messed up and drove drunk to Taco Bell, and she just felt like shit or something on the lines of that. Once she saw Maggie and Amaya, the truth came out. One of her exes was in town and they were at the bar Mingles. After Brody and all of them were done for the night, she went and picked him up and they went back to his hotel. She told Maggie and Amaya it was the best sex of her life—big shock; clearly, she tells everybody that. Also, keep in mind that this is all while I'm in Oregon, and she's texting me, "I love you so much," "I miss you," and "I'm gonna marry you." *What the fuck!!* That shit's crazy! What kind of sick fucker could do that!? Amaya and Maggie told Alexis that she needed to tell me, but she told them she'll just wait till closer to graduation and break up with me for the exact reason of graduation and life after.

As I hear all of this, so much anger and sadness come over me. I bite my lips on the inside of my mouth, talking to myself in my head so I don't bawl my eyes out in front of everybody. They told me more, but it was all close to the same thing. They talked about how she cheated on her last boyfriend, but they thought this time was different because of the way she acted with me, but I guess not.

I went home and told Dalton, Kade, and Kiara. Kade, we'll just say, he had some kind words about her. Dalton and Kiara were in shock and didn't really know what to say. The next week was about to be the worst thing I've been through since the Norco incident. I was talking with Dalton a lot every day about why somebody would do such a thing to a person. He gave me great advice, and we had a lot of good laughs together during the talks. But at the end of the day, it was still me, and now I was in my head more than ever. I was calling out of work because mentally I was fucked up and couldn't be at work. I went to beach volleyball with Dalton, which was one of the many things we were great at, and it helped me keep my mind off everything.

That's when I got a text from her that asked, "How are you?" Then it all went back to shit. Also, just so all of you know, she still had no clue that I knew what she did. Dalton told me to just leave it and play, which we did. Overall, that was a great day, and I was with one of the people who meant the most to me in my life, which made it a lot better.

The next few days were just as bad as the others. I would wake up and feel dead. I was a literal zombie. I didn't care about anything in life or about life itself for that whole week. My whole family knew at this point so they kept checking up on me. And I was texting Brody, Amaya, and Maggie all the time, which just ate me up inside because their best friend was the person that broke me, and they were still hanging out with her but trying to help me at the same time. Even though I didn't put them in a bad spot, I felt like I was. It felt like a pity party to me because I was just the ex-boyfriend and not as close to them as Alexis was. So I would apologize to them for always texting them, but of course, they were good people, so they didn't care.

I wanted to text Alexis so bad and ask her why she would do such a thing. But I knew I couldn't because it would ruin her friendship with Maggie and Amaya. But not texting her was also ruining me. During the week, nights were the hardest because I was alone, and that meant I would use my brain even more but not for good things.

One of the nights, I was really mad and my heart hurt. I was thinking I'm really not going to do a thing with my life, YouTube's a joke that'll never happen, I don't have a future at all, and maybe that's why she cheated on me. I was ruining myself all because of her, and I wanted to blame what I was thinking on her. But I couldn't because the pain was from her but what I did with it was on me.

I had pain pills that didn't have the side effects of Norco. You see, with Norco, when you took enough, your ears would almost feel plugged up to the point where you could barely hear at certain times. The reason for that is because you were so high that it felt like blood was rushing through your brain. It felt warm, and when I felt like that, I was so numb I didn't have any worries. I would just lay down and pass out. Of course, waking up was a scary thing because I knew I was gonna throw my guts up. But being numb for those thirty-five minutes was worth it to me.

This time I took a pill called meloxicam. I was looking up the pill to see if it would give me the same high as Norco did. Once I typed in "meloxicam side effects," a bunch of different things popped up and not a single one I was thrilled about. The heavy hitters were: increase in heart attack; holes in stomach or intestine; internal bleeding; and blood clots or stroke.

I was not happy with the results of my research, and guess what my stupid ass did!? I was only supposed to take two a day, one in the morning and one at night, and I wasn't even taking them because I didn't need them anymore. Here I was at night, eating myself alive, and I put about six in my hand, grabbed the Patron from my drawer, and took about a fifteen-second chug with the pills going down my throat like water. I still couldn't sleep, so after a little bit I rolled over and popped four more, but this time with water, which was so much better.

Here I was popping pills, knowing I could die. I talk to God, begging him to keep me alive while I cry my eyes out. What gives me the fucking right!! I read the side effects and knew there was a possibility I wouldn't wake up, and yet I still did it. And for what reason? Because of a fucking girl!? A girl who never cared about me in the first place, a girl who threw away our relationship, a girl who lied to my face the entire time. And I was gonna throw my whole life away because of that!! Then I agreed with everything I was saying to myself. I was hurt so bad and I was so tired of fighting. I'd already gotten out of the dark pit I was in before, and it took a lot to get out of it so I didn't wanna do it again. I didn't wanna fight anymore. I was heartbroken because I thought she was the one. But then I realized I also thought Alyx was the one. The reason I was so heartbroken was because for the first time in my life, I was comfortable, content, happy—whatever you wanna call it—and she took all of that away. She looked me in the eye and I believed everything that came out of that mouth. I thought I read her like a book, and I was so far from right. She played me from the beginning, and that's why I was so heartbroken. Yet again, here I was popping pills all because of some stupid girl.

The morning came and thankfully I woke up. That morning was horrible. I woke up and cried my eyes out until I couldn't. It was the first time since I was about seven that I couldn't breathe because I was crying so hard. All I could think about were all of the good things with Alexis, and it hurt me to the core that she did what she did. After a little while, Dalton and I talked as he helped in the best way he could. I didn't tell him about the pills, but I told him what I was thinking as I started to cry, which I hated doing in front of people because it made me feel weak. He was tearing up a little bit but stayed strong, we just talked for a little bit and then I called out of work and stayed in bed for most of the day because I was so exhausted from my own mind.

Dalton was heading back home to Oregon so it was just going to be Kade, Kiara, and me, so we were going out to the bars a few times. I was also hanging out with Spencer a lot more, which was nice. But in that week, I consumed more alcohol than I ever had. I was talking like four days in a row. I was drunker than Donny Burger. One of the nights, I was drunk, and guess what I fucking did? I texted the devil herself, Alexis! I was sad and drunk, and those are the two things that should never go together. I texted her as if I was so happy and wanting to talk with her, which she didn't think was a very good idea. But I convinced her, and she came over to pick me up. I didn't really know what my plan was, but I just wanted her to admit what she did and do my best to not bring up what I actually know.

We went back to the Top of the World where we started to talk. It was slow at first. I started by asking about why we broke up because the reasoning to me didn't make sense, which I was right about the whole time now that I know what actually happened!! She said the same shit she said before. But then I stopped her and said, "There was never another guy involved?" She responded confidently with a firm "No." I knew she was lying so I kept consistent on what the real reason was.

That's when she said this, which, before I get into it, once she said this, it took everything in my power to not just tell her everything I knew. It made me more mad than I was before!! I bought her a bunch of gifts or dinner or whatever because that was just what I wanted to do for her. Just bringing this up for context. She said the other reason we broke up was because, and I quote, "My family never really liked you, which is a really big problem for me, and when it comes to money, I think it could be a problem in the future because you got me these things."

I just stood there in awe and didn't really know what to say. But what I wanted to say was: "Bitch, I'm fucking twenty-one years old, and, yeah, I'm not rich. Also, motherfucker, you needed help paying for your house like last month! Sitting here talking to me about money, maaaannn, *fuck you*!!" But that was also drunk me in my head talking.

We kissed a couple of times which was a God-awful idea, but it happened. At the end of the conversation, I brought up one more thing to see if she would come clean about what she did. There was a girl who always came into my work. Her brother did too, but I talked with her more. One of the days I was at work, I looked really down, so she asked me if I was OK, and then I told her the news. She said, "Oh yeah, you were dating Alexis, right!?" It threw me off because I never told her my girlfriend's (now ex-girlfriend's) name. Her brother found out I was dating her because one of his best friends was Alexis's ex. She told me her brother thought it was bad news I was dating her, but he didn't say anything because he assumed she changed. But she cheated on her last boyfriend when she always told me he cheated. That was why she knew her name because apparently around certain people, she didn't have a very good reputation.

I brought it up in the conversation, and her whole tone changed. She was crying most of the time we were talking. I wanted to feel bad for her 'cause I didn't like seeing her cry. But then I was wondering why she was crying, like, why the fuck is she crying!? But ya know, the Oscar goes to!! Anyway, as soon as I brought that up, she stopped crying and was acting confused. All she said was: "No, I would never do that. I already told you what happened!" After that conversation, I didn't have anything else in the tank to ask her because whatever she did tell me, I wasn't going to believe it. At this point, I didn't know what the truth and what the lies were. So, she dropped me off and that was that!

The next day, I was at work and still in a shitty mood because although I wanted to just move on right away, I couldn't. I loved her even though she did all of that. Of course, it helped in getting over her faster, but I was still hurting. I was at work and I got a text from her that said, "WE NEED TO TALK! I am so pissed right now!" While I was having this conversation at work, there was some girl eavesdropping, and her friend worked with Alexis. So, the whole time I was talking about my relationship that ended, she was texting her friend a bunch of bullshit, and it pissed Alexis off. She was looking at my location, telling me she was just gonna text this random girl who came into the gym, and I was starting to freak the fuck out. I told Alexis I would talk with her after work.

I called Maggie and Amaya and told them about the situation, which they thought was fucking crazy. I also told them that I was gonna tell Alexis I knew about everything. They were not big fans of my plan because it would ruin the friendship that they had with her, and it would ruin the friendship I had with them. But I told them what kind of person would lie about everything the entire time and then get involved with people at my work just to cover up their tracks because they know that everything that's being said about them is true? That is fucking crazy to me! They didn't have any words, and they just told me I shouldn't meet up with her.

Work finally ended, and I finally started to stop shaking, but now I had a big decision to make. I could either tell Alexis I knew everything and blow up her world but also mine and everyone else's, or I could talk with her and have her lie through her teeth while looking me in the eyes again. One sounded a lot better than the other, and I was sick of being the nice guy, so I would make a last-minute decision once I saw her. I picked her up and we drove around while she was talking the whole time about a bunch of shit that I told her wasn't true. That was basically the conversation. Once I pulled into the parking lot to drop her off, it was now my time to make a decision. I hesitated when I looked at her and said, "Alexis, odds are I might not ever see you again, so do you have anything else you wanna tell me?" She took a second and responded with, "Nope, that's all of it!" She left and that was that. I wanted to tell her so bad that I knew so that maybe the next guy that falls for her like I did wouldn't get hurt because she would've got a wake-up call. But I didn't want to ruin Maggie and Amaya's friendship with her, so I left it alone.

I wanted to forget about her and block her, but a fire was lit inside of me, and I wanted her to watch me succeed! Even though this fire was lit, I couldn't stay steady on YouTube because I wasn't in the right mind space to make videos. I was becoming closer with everybody else, which was really nice. We were doing things all the time, which drained my bank account fast. But at this point, I didn't care because I was feeling happy.

We were going to the bars a lot, and it grossed me out because of how easy it was. I know that sounds fucked, but then Alexis came to mind, and I was just imagining her and how easy she really was. I know that sounds fucked up, but what she did was way worse, so I think a few mean words are OK. What I mean by "easy" is I could have gone home with any girl that night. The way some of them look at you or act toward you, it was crazy to me that it was that easy. Also, I'm not going to lie to you, I wanted to go home with some of these girls or have them come home with me because I missed the sex and everything else that came with it.

But I couldn't do it, because although I'll pop pills, I'm not a total douchebag to just fuck a girl and go on to the next. That's where I draw the line, and that's when I started to realize that it was for the best that she dumped me because it was a dead-end relationship that wasn't going to go anywhere. Now, yeah, I thought I was gonna marry her, but it was filled with a bunch of lies from her and no respect from her. Usually I would be at fault a little for a breakup, but not this time! Whatever I was to do was never going to be good enough, and she was always going to seek more even if I was perfect to her, which I already was. It didn't matter.

With that realization, it hurt. But, as the saying goes, "It is what it is," and there wasn't a thing I could do about it. So

I had to do my best to learn to let go of her. Even though it's easier said than done, I was taking a step in the right direction. The big thing I did to help me move in the right direction even more was to text her brother about what happened. I really enjoyed being around her family even though we had our differences. I thought her brother was a really cool kid, and I didn't want him to think I was some asshole. I didn't know what she was telling him so I told him everything to clear the air, and after doing that, I felt a little better. I started having a thing with a girl named Kendall who was part of Spencer's friend group, which came out of nowhere. I didn't think I would be ready to talk to someone else but I actually liked her! We hung out a few times but she just wanted to be friends, and I respected that, so that's what we are. I still wasn't too persistent on YouTube like I used to be, but I was feeling good being around great people so I was doing my best to not beat myself up about it! After the situation that happened, I was low on funds. I thought about going home for the summer to stack up some cash so I wouldn't stress as much and have funds for YouTube, which was my dream, and certain funds to try to travel more!

FINAL CHAPTER

Time for a One on One

Now, that last chapter that you just read about my ex and how she broke me into a million pieces happened around April 28, 2023. As I'm writing this, it's May 22, 2023, so yeah that didn't happen very long ago! But by the time all of you are reading this, it could be a very long time ago. Right now, I'm in Moscow, Idaho, but I'm going home for the summer to stack up cash, like I was saying.

This book is called *The Midlife Crisis of a Nineteen-Year-Old*. I am now twenty-one years old and guess what? I don't have life figured out! I know that with how good looking I sound and with how well-spoken I may be, it comes as a shock to a lot of you. But, yeah, I don't have it figured out. And guess what? It's OK that I don't have it figured out. If anyone tells you they have it figured out, they're lying unless it's like Jeff Bezos or Steve Jobs. Then, ya know, I would take whatever advice they give you.

But everyone in this world has a plan. And even if you don't have a plan, that's OK because that's the whole point of getting a plan in the first place—you don't have one. There are a lot of things people want to do in this world and they won't ever do them. I know that's a fucking killer of a sentence but it's true! Whether it has to do with fear, money, time, or opinions, people will fold. When it comes to time, we don't have enough of it. When it comes to money, we also don't have enough of it. But when it comes to fear, now, that's something you can control. Now, if you're afraid of snakes, I'm not gonna tell you to jump in a pit of snakes. That's just fucking stupid! But when it comes to that girl you wanna talk to, the music you wanna make, the places you wanna explore, starting a YouTube channel like me, or whatever it may be—*why not?*!

What's the thing that scares you the most about going after something that you want? Is it the possibility that you might fail, or, sorry, not *might* fail, but that you *will* fail? You're going to fail the first time you do something new or do something out of your comfort zone. But if you don't fail, then you're not even trying! You have to fail in life in order to experience life. I'm a prime example of this. I beat myself up mentally because sometimes I feel like a failure to my family, friends, ex-girlfriends, or whatever else. I mean I have literally tried to end my life to get rid of that failure. But imagine if one of those times I tried, it worked. I would have hurt so many people because I thought life was too hard, and I wasn't doing anything with it so I gave up.

In order to truly experience the highs in life, you're gonna have to go through the lows. I'm not saying pop pills or anything like that. Please, don't do that! When it comes to heartbreak, failure, or mental illness, these are going to be some of the greatest killers to you of all time. You're gonna wanna give up or give in to your thoughts and do the things that you don't want to. But since you're so tired of fighting, you're gonna give in, or when it comes to heartbreak, you might wanna get even or feed off the pain that the one person gave you. I think feeding off that pain is a good thing for a very little amount of time because you can work out all of the anger that you feel toward that person or maybe even use it as motivation. But if you keep feeding off that pain, it's going to turn into a lot more than that. When it comes to revenge, for example, you doing something or working for something just to make that person jealous, you can't do that! If you do that, then you're not doing anything for yourself. You're doing it to try and impress the person that did you wrong so you can hurt their feelings. Also, news flash, if you do end up doing that, then that person wins because now they know that you still care about them. The only reason you're doing the things you're doing is to spite them.

Forgiveness is a really powerful thing, and it is so fucking hard to do! For instance, when it comes to Alexis, I still love her. And as dumb as it sounds, if she came back to me, I would probably jump on that opportunity in a flat second. But then I realized all the things she did and the pain she caused me, and I say no way, fuck her! She did me wrong so I'm gonna do her wrong! But really, I don't wanna do that. I just get upset about the situation.

Now, here's the thing. I'm not one to talk because I still haven't fully forgiven her for what she did to me, but I still want the best for her! I still think she's an amazing person and that she can do great things, and I hope she does. I just hope she doesn't do that to another person. Like I was saying, I know forgiving a person for what they did is easier said than done. But everybody in this world is going to make mistakes or do things that hurt you, whether it's big or little. If you held onto all of those, you would be a horrible person. No offense, but it's true.

There are going to be so many people in this world who are gonna do their best to drag you down. Whenever someone tries to step out of the ordinary and do something different, people start reacting in bad ways because they can't wrap their little minds around your idea. Everybody in this world has a dream, and it's all up to you on whether or not you're gonna reach it.

Now, yes, life happens, and sometimes you're gonna have to stop putting so much time into that dream you have because life comes at us fast and you have responsibilities. But that doesn't mean you just completely forget about that dream! If it's something you always think about and you're not doing it for money, fame, or whatever it may be, but you're doing it because you actually love it with everything you have, then the world is yours! You can reach whatever goal you want as long as you want it badly enough and work hard enough.

Believing in yourself is one of the hardest things to do, especially when life gets hard and you're always down on yourself. When things do get hard, I know all of you wanna stay strong and not ask for any help. But that is so important because if you're like me, you don't wanna ask. But then you bottle up all your emotions until one day you do something like pop a bunch of pills or try to do other things to harm yourself. So, when life gets hard, don't be scared to be open with the people around you. For me, if my uncle wasn't home when I got home from popping the Xanax, I wouldn't be writing this right now.

A lot of things happen within a day, and sometimes, one moment could piss you off so much or ruin your day. But don't let it happen. Yeah, I know, once again, easier said than done. But don't let ten bad minutes in a day ruin your entire day! What happened is now in the past, and if there was nothing you could do about it, you can't be pissed off!

Yeah, I fuck this up all the time. I mean, just about how I got cheated on, I didn't do a fucking thing, but yet here I am ruining my days because of it. But I can't, and neither should you, because some things you just don't have control over! If you do keep dwelling on the past, then you're digging your own grave. The more and more you do it, the faster your mental health is going to decline. At that point, you single-handedly ruined yourself. If you're so focused on the past, how could you ever truly experience the moment you're in right now!? Oh yeah, you can't experience it because you only dwell on the past. Then you're going to hurt even more because life flew right by you, and you didn't even realize all of the great things happening. Don't do that! I mean, I would say more about that, but that's about it. Just don't fucking do that!

Sadness and depression are two very different things. Some of you might be saying, "No shit." But I'm saying this because although a lot of people in the world are depressed, I feel like the word "depression" gets thrown around like the word "hey!" If you have a bad week or a bad day, you're not depressed. I may sound like an asshole because, yeah, who am I to tell you what you're feeling!? But that's just the truth. Sadness is just little moments in your life that can put you in a shitty mood for a couple days or, hell, maybe even a couple weeks! I know somebody could be sad for even a couple months, but it's what comes with that sadness that could either be depression or just sadness. They are both really shitty things. I'm not undermining one or the other, but they are very different things.

In my own words, I'm going to give you my best explanation of depression. I already said that sadness is just little moments that you can dwell on for a bit but then they go away over time. Depression can also go away over time but here's the difference. Depression is a deadly thing because out around your friends, you'll have lots of laughs and smiles. But as soon as you have time alone, you're fucked. Once your mind is not occupied, it becomes occupied on how much it hates you, you hating yourself. Basically, look at it as sadness but instead of trying to be happier, you gave in to the sadness, and you let it consume you because you were too tired to keep going. Depression is a scary thing because it takes over your mind. Once you are depressed, you give in to a lot of things that aren't good for you or you give in to things that are easier than something else because it's too much work for you to do. Once again, bad for you. With depression, that's why you have to rely on people close to you sometimes. If you don't, you'll bury yourself deeper and deeper until you can't get out as easily—if you get out at all.

I wanna do my best to help you guys with your mental health problems. That's the main reason I wrote this book. I know what it's like to feel so alone even though you have everyone in your corner or to not wanna wake up the next day. Even though you know that's wrong to think, it's how you feel! Life is always going to be hard. A lot of people say life gets easier, and I do believe that one day, dreams change. You find that special someone and everything with them is your dream because that's all you want in life. But even then, life will have its amazing moments and it will have its horrible moments! Life will get easier, but it depends on what you will do with yours. No one can tell you, "Life gets easier, so don't worry," because everyone has very different lives. I'm here to try to help, and your family and friends are there to help. But it doesn't matter what anyone says or does because it's always going to be you against yourself. Life will get easier as long as you don't lose to yourself, but it takes a lot of failing to learn to not give up. As long as you keep getting up, you're going to feel a lot better mentally because you've been at the lowest and you can still get up. Just remember to keep having that mindset!

If I had to leave you with anything, I'll just say this. Always be kind. You have no idea what anyone in this world is going through, and you have the power to either make or break somebody with your actions. Always, and I mean always, *love hard!* Now this one is a bitch because for me it's going to be hard on the next relationship because of you-know-who but...I say always love hard and don't put up walls because heartbreak will happen whether you wanna believe it or you don't, it always will! When you find that person that you really like or love, you can't have any walls up because both of you are taking time out of your lives to get to know one another. That's very important, and if you aren't fully honest with them, that's not fair to you or the other person. Odds are that it won't work because you never opened up to that person so they could see the true you. A lot of you are scared of heartbreak because it hurts—OMG, it fucking hurts—but that's the whole point of life! You have to learn what works and what doesn't, what you like and what you don't like. If you're the person who says, "Well, Hunter, what if it doesn't work?" then I would tell you *"What if it does?!"* You won't have a clue if you never take the jump!

Also, don't just love hard to your significant other but you should love everyone close to you with all of your heart! If people in your life mean that much to you, then you should remind them because sometimes they get worried about life or down on themselves too, and they'll need you in their corner!

Family and friends are some of the most important people you can have in your life, and things happen as you grow older that will make it to where you're not as close. But do your best to stay in touch with everybody because those are the people who will always be there for you and who you need the most, so don't ever take that for granted.

Sometimes, friends are closer than family because you tell them things more than your own parents! I couldn't even imagine going a day without my parents or my brother. Although I'm really close to them and all of my friends, if it wasn't for Dalton, I'm not sure if I would be here. That's why it's important to try and keep everyone close and open up to people!

Never stress about money! I know that is a crazy-ass thing to say, even for me because I stress about money all the time, but do your best not to! I know you need money to live or do fun things, and I know money is the thing that makes the world go round, but it's also the killer of all. Once you start stressing about money, it can take away all of your happiness. It's not going to be an easy thing to not stress about, but just do the best you can!

Stay out of your comfort zone! There are so many things none of us wants to do in life. But once you can teach yourself to get up and do those things that you don't like, it'll make you such a stronger person. By doing this, you're opening a door to a lot more opportunity because you have the guts to keep going!

This is the biggest one of them all! Always, and I mean for eternity, always love yourself. Now a lot of people say you should learn to love yourself before you can get in a relationship and love somebody else. But to be honest, I don't always agree with that statement because sometimes you need somebody else to show you that love because you've never known how to love yourself. Loving yourself is an important thing to do, be easier on yourself, congratulate yourself for little achievements! You may have not reached your end goal of what you want, but you have to give yourself a pat on the back for working toward something and achieving things!

If you don't like the way your body looks or if you don't think you're attractive, every single person has different genes when it comes to their body so just know that everybody's body is unique in its own way. There are certain things that you have that another person might not so they want what you have or vice versa. Be comfortable in your own skin because that's what makes people beautiful, the uniqueness in everyone.

Now if you don't think you're attractive, then you should stop thinking that because there is somebody out there for all of us. Being attractive isn't all about the way you look. I mean, shit, prime example is my ex. I mean damn! She was a *smoke show*, and now that I know the true her, I think she's a horrible person and very unattractive because of it. Just have confidence in yourself and you're going to be just fine!

Loving yourself can save your life and other people's lives, and just know that every day you wake up you impact so many people's lives for just being you! So, keep being you and keep dreaming big because that's all life's about!! Just know that the sun is a daily reminder that all of us can rise even after being in the dark for so long!

If any of you have stories you wanna tell me or you just need somebody you can talk to, you can email me here:
Huntercarter307@gmail.com

Thank you all for reading, and never give up on yourselves!

"The giant in front of us is never bigger than the God inside of us."
John 4:4

Made in United States
Troutdale, OR
02/05/2024